THE MENEHUNE OF POLYNESIA AND OTHER MYTHICAL LITTLE PEOPLE OF OCEANIA

BY

KATHARINE LUOMALA

COACHWHIP PUBLICATIONS

Greenville, Ohio

The Menehune of Polynesia, by Katharine Luomala
© 2013 Coachwhip Publications
Front cover: Parrot Heliconia © Pixbox77
No claims made on public domain material.
Published 1951 as Bulletin 203 for the Bishop Museum.

ISBN 1-61646-214-0
ISBN-13 978-1-61646-214-7

CoachwhipBooks.com

CONTENTS

CONTENTS

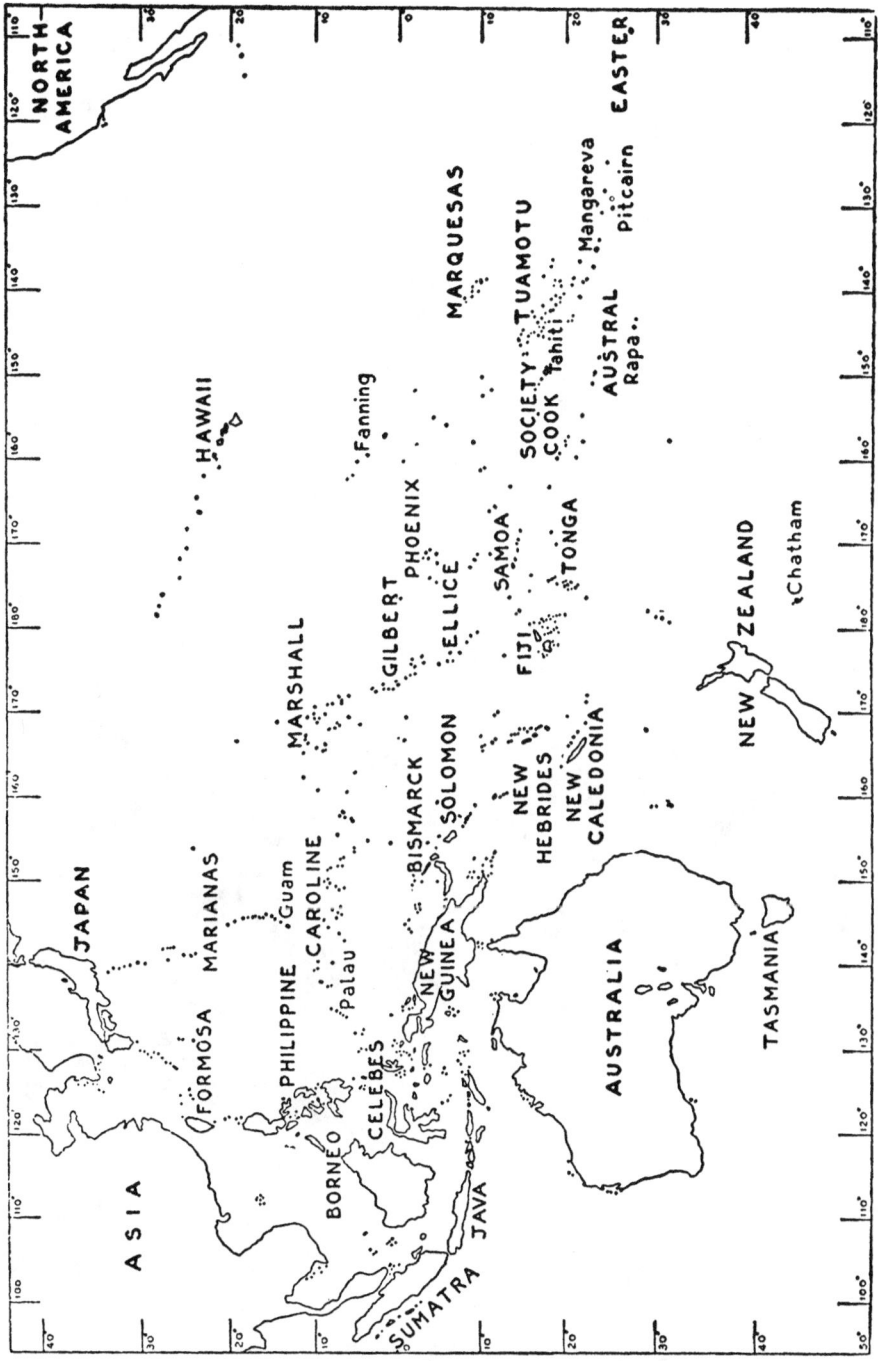

NORTH AMERICA

ASIA

JAPAN

FORMOSA

PHILIPPINE

BORNEO

CELEBES

SUMATRA

JAVA

MARIANAS

Guam

CAROLINE

Palau

NEW GUINEA

BISMARCK

SOLOMON

NEW HEBRIDES

NEW CALEDONIA

AUSTRALIA

TASMANIA

MARSHALL

GILBERT

ELLICE

FIJI

SAMOA

TONGA

PHOENIX

Fanning

HAWAII

MARQUESAS

TUAMOTU

SOCIETY

Tahiti

COOK

AUSTRAL

Rapa

Mangareva

Pitcairn

EASTER

NEW ZEALAND

Chatham

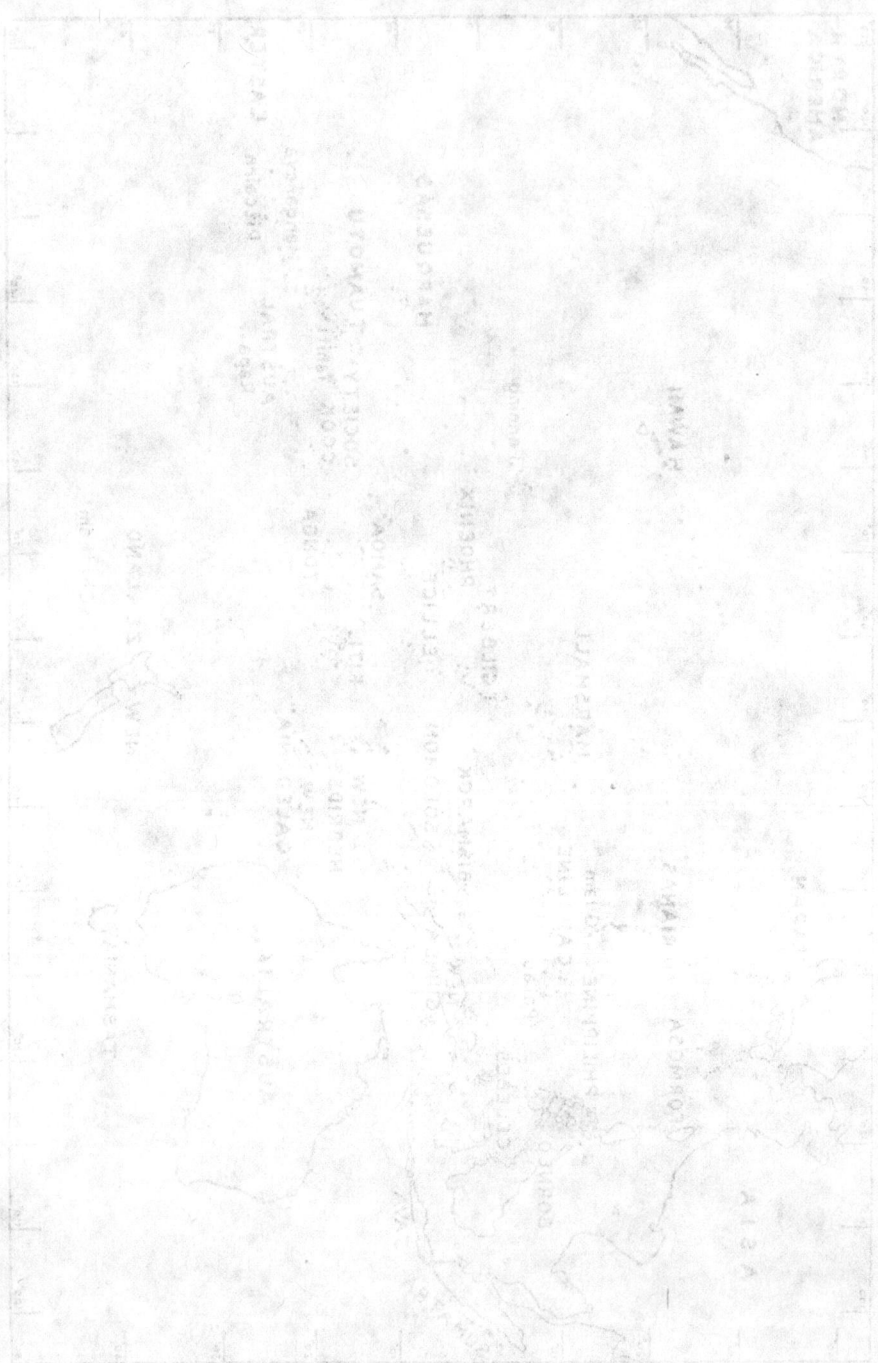

The Menehune of Polynesia and other Mythical Little People of Oceania

By KATHARINE LUOMALA

INTRODUCTION

Scope of Study

The night-working dwarfs, or Menehune, and the volcano goddess, Pele, compete today in the Hawaiian Islands for first place in popular interest in local folklore. To many children, regardless of racial or social or intellectual group, Menehune still live in the islands. Belief in their existence appears to persist even past the age when a belief in Santa Claus has been surrendered. One encounters adults, educated and presumably sane individuals, who become quite indignant if an eyebrow is twitched about their belief in the Menehune. Few of these believing children of all ages have a drop of Hawaiian blood.

Until after World War II, it scarcely occurred to anyone to commercialize the Menehune beyond taking tourists to see the Oahu fishponds said to have been built by the little people in one night. However, during the last two or three years, the energetic Menehune have been lured to the main business streets and put to work as salesmen. A Menehune maiden has been trapped, given a Hollywood glamour treatment, draped in a brief sarong to satisfy modern modesty, given a teen-age hair style resembling the bobbed tail of a horse, and set to exploiting the charms of rayon and nylon lingerie. Her fat brother extols the wonders of candy; a cousin sells automobiles. Thus far, Menehune friends have not organized to protect this minority, but a Menehune Protective Society would have plenty of work to investigate these little people who claim to be Menehune but work in the daylight instead of at night and who have abandoned their old crafts of temple and road building.

In this article, material from various parts of the Pacific which may help in understanding the Hawaiian Menehune is summarized, analyzed, and compared. Included are stories, beliefs, and scientific theories concerning three categories of beings: (1) the Hawaiian Menehune and related types in Hawaii; (2) groups of people in central Polynesia called Manahune or Manaune, terms which are dialectical variants of the name Menehune; and (3) dwarfs or pygmies in several Pacific island mythologies who, though not called Menehune, have certain resemblances to them. This survey may give a new perspective on the identity of the Menehune described in the collections of myths by Fornander, Rice, and Thrum; their origin; and, particularly, the reason for the existence of Menehune.

William Hyde Rice describes the Menehune as "A race of mythical dwarfs from two to three feet in height, who were possessed of great strength; a race of pygmies who were squat, tremendously strong, powerfully built, and very ugly of face. They were credited with the building of many temples, roads, and other structures. Trades among them were well-systematized, every Menehune being restricted to his own particular craft in which he was a master. It was believed that they would work only one night on a construction and if unable to complete the work, it was left undone." (See Rice, 52, p. 136.) [1]

Those who regard the Menehune as their favorite characters in Hawaiian mythology may resent any attempt to analyze these appealing little beings, and may say that anyone who would dissect a hapless Menehune caught in the scientific net would pick the wings off butterflies. With bowed head, the scientist can only point out in defense that he is not satisfied with mere contemplation of the wonders of the world but inevitably finds his admiration leading to analysis. His point of view is dynamic, not static. Aside from the personal interest of the scientist in satisfying his curiosity about the Menehune and their other admirers, additional reasons make the dissection worthwhile.

The present beliefs about the Menehune and the older myths about them represent an end product of human imagination in Hawaii, both of natives and of foreigners. The only way to find out why people think up beings like the Menehune or tell such stories about them as are told is to study the creators and the objects of their creation. Belief in the Menehune is not a static, dying tradition. Technically, it is what anthropologists call a cultural survival, or retention. When a belief, custom, or object of an earlier age lingers into a later period but acquires a new meaning or context, it is called a survival. Modern Hawaii has inherited the belief in the Menehune from old Hawaii. The belief continues to live, grow, and change.

As people in Hawaii know, it is customary to speak of the Menehune as the real *kamaʻaina* of the Hawaiian Islands. The term *kamaʻaina* means, literally, "child of the land," and connotes the native-born of the islands. By extension, it has come to mean aborigines. According to present-day folk belief, which seems to exist on every social and educational level, the Menehune are the aborigines of the islands. In this particular frame of reference, the Menehune are regarded as real people who belong to *Homo sapiens*. Side by side, often in the mind of one individual, the Menehune are regarded as supernatural beings. People who feel a need to explain the two conflicting points of view say either that the Menehune were real people who, with the passage of time, have been folklorized by later arrivals in the land, or that they are supernatural beings to whom the deeds of real people were ascribed after the history of the deeds had been forgotten. It is one of the problems of this paper to give the evidence for such explanations.

---

[1] Numbers in parentheses refer to the Bibliography, page 85.

The influence of the folk belief in the Menehune as real people, aborigines of the islands, is evident, as we shall see, in anthropological studies attempting to reconstruct the pre-European history of the Hawaiian Islands. We must examine any evidence there may be to warrant using the term in this way in scientific reports.

This same folk belief has achieved sociological significance in the Hawaii of today. If the Menehune are the true *kama'aina,* then everyone else in the islands is a *malihini*—a stranger, a foreigner, a newcomer—a term with derogatory connotations. The *malihini* or his ancestors missed the first double canoe eastward, the name of which is unknown though in this modern argument it ranks in prestige with the *Mayflower.* However, there was another ship, the *Thaddeus,* more important locally than the *Mayflower,* which in 1820 brought missionaries of the American Board of Commissioners for Foreign Missions to the islands. Popular usage designates these missionaries and their descendants as the *kama'aina* too. Then there are those of various racial origins who are unconnected with this group but claim to be *kama'aina* because they were born in the islands. A variant system, which enhances the prestige of a greater number of other people, is to label as *kama'aina* those who have been here a certain number of months or years, or have achieved a certain condition epitomized in the popular saying, "When the iron in your blood turns to lead in your pants, you're a *kama'aina.*"

The Menehune were forcibly reintroduced into this long-term, low-level sniping between the *kama'aina* and the *malihini* during the strikes of 1946, when union leaders were labeled *malihini,* among other terms, by their opponents. A widely publicized retort was that only the Menehune could claim to be *kama'aina.* But were the Menehune, as I have asked before, real people; and if they were, were they the aborigines of the islands? I propose to throw the question wide open, even at the risk of opening old wounds. The Menehune should have a fair deal too. They have been a political football long enough. It is time that people stopped bandying their name about in name-calling feuds.

In central Polynesia (the Society and Cook Islands and the Tuamotus), the word Manahune, related linguistically to Menehune, is the name of certain groups of people. Who are these groups? What relation, if any, is there between them and the Hawaiian Menehune? And in many parts of Polynesia and in the adjoining island areas of Micronesia and Melanesia are myths, traditions, and beliefs about little people who are reminiscent of the Menehune although called by other names. Also clustering about local characters other than the little people of these areas are certain myths which recall the Hawaiian beliefs about the Menehune. For instance, like the Hawaiian Menehune, these characters are believed to work only at night and to be invisible by day. Comparable beliefs elsewhere in the world about nocturnal-working, little people, who may have been aborigines of the land, are outside the scope of this paper.

SOURCE MATERIAL ON THE MENEHUNE

What kind of evidence is there about the Menehune in which to seek answers, however tentative, to the questions asked?

Polynesian natives had no writing before Europeans introduced the art. Consequently, there are no histories of the islands which date from before European discovery. Traditions were handed down orally from generation to generation. All the written data belong to one time level, the European, and cover only the last 355 years (the first historical reference to a Polynesian island appears in the journal of Mendaña, who discovered the Marquesas in 1595). Much of the coverage is inadequate even for the historic period.

There is, then, no pre-European written history of the Menehune either. Written records about them in Hawaii date back about a half century, in central Polynesia, about 180 years. These documents include two categories of information: (1) traditions, genealogies, beliefs, and customs relating to the Menehune that were current at the time Europeans or natives first began to write them down; and (2) fairly recent beliefs connecting the Menehune with archeological sites such as ruins of heiaus (temples), fishponds, and unusual rocks or piles of rocks.

Although the recorders may, in good faith, have regarded some of their information as ancient and as having been handed down orally and unchanged generation after generation, scientists of today place little confidence in such information as a source of direct history. However, they use it as an indirect source in attempting to reconstruct Polynesian history of the preliterate period. Such reconstructions admittedly represent history based on inference. They are tentative, and indicate only what might have occurred.

Nearly all the material about the Menehune comes from Rice's account in "Hawaiian legends" (52) and from the stories and descriptions contributed to the Hawaiian Annual by J. H. Kaiwi, John M. Lydgate, and the editor, Thomas G. Thrum, who also translated Kaiwi's story (42, pp. 114-118). Thrum writes that his interest in the little people won him the title of "the father of the Menehunes" (70, p. 83).

Other articles in the Hawaiian Annual on the Menehune and related peoples of small stature are: [Thomas G. Thrum], "Stories of the Menehunes" (62, pp. 112-117); John M. Lydgate, "The affairs of the Wainiha Hui" (44, pp. 125-137); [Thomas G. Thrum], "The legend of Kanehuna-moku" (67, pp. 140-147); J. H. Kaiwi, "Story of the race of Menehunes of Kauai" (42, pp. 114-118); J. M. Lydgate, "Legend of the floating island" (46, pp. 134-137); Thomas G. Thrum, "Who or what were the Menehunes" (70, pp. 83-88). The last article incorporates material from items listed above and from scattered references to Menehune in the following of Thrum's papers in the same series: "Manoa Valley" (61, pp. 110-116); "Heiaus and heiau sites throughout the

Hawaiian Islands" (65, pp. 36-48, 1907; pp. 38-43, 1909); and "Tales from the temples" (64, pp. 49-69, 1907; pp. 44-54, 1909); and from "Heiaus (temples) of Hawaii Nei" (69, pp. 14-36). Thrum reprinted some of his material on Menehune in "Hawaiian folk tales" (63, pp. 107-117); "Hawaiian traditions: Stories of the Menehunes" (66) and "More Hawaiian folk tales" (68, pp. 214-219). The Journal of the Polynesian Society (42) printed his translation of Kaiwi's article with text.

Abraham Fornander refers to the Menehune occasionally in his two great works (26, vol. 1, pp. 55, 98, 99; vol. 2, pp. 6, 23; vol. 3, p. 132 and vol. 27, pp. 226, 270-272, 277, 349). Menehune appear in two of Laura Green's stories (31, pp. 70-79), and Westervelt's anthologies (71, pp. 116-151; 72, pp. 5-6, 131-132) also have references to them. Martha W. Beckwith devotes a chapter to reviewing the source material on the Menehune and related peoples in her study of Hawaiian mythology (5, pp. 321-326). Popular rewrites need not concern us here, since they do not represent folk inventions.

References to Menehune also appear in manuscripts written by both Hawaiians and Caucasians and stored at Bishop Museum, and some of this material is incorporated into my study. The earliest reference to the Menehune which I have found in the translated and dated manuscripts is 1885.

The frequent repetition of material from the collections of Rice, Thrum, and Fornander does not mean that new data about the Menehune are no longer obtainable. It means, rather, that folk beliefs which still circulate about the little people have not been written down; that some written collections have not been published; or that too often new material is so jazzed up by the collector before publication that it has no scientific value, in that one is unable to separate native tradition from the collector's interpretations and elaborations. Also, many people tend to feel that if their Menehune myths are not obtained from an elderly Hawaiian who claims to have heard them from his grandfather or grandmother, they are of no value. However, one should not limit the search for Menehune stories to narrators of Hawaiian descent, for the Menehune have been incorporated into folk beliefs of other races in the Hawaiian Islands of today. A Menehune myth adopted and retold by, say, a Filipino plantation worker and accepted as a part of the folk beliefs in his community is valuable source material, for the history of his retold version can be traced and the processes of adoption and acculturation studied. Important as the continuous collecting of data from old Hawaiians is, collectors are missing an opportunity to study the birth and growth of myths by not recording the stories and beliefs of the many other peoples now living in the islands.

A friend of Japanese descent on the island of Kauai, with which the Menehune are particularly closely identified, tells me that her parents used the Menehune as bogeymen to frighten her into being a good girl when she was small. She and her friends lived in dread of meeting a Menehune, let alone a band of them, and hurried to get home before dark, when the little people are believed to be on their way to work. Another friend tells me that a few years ago children attending school at Waimea, Kauai, believed that some Menehune hung about the school ground and ran under the building when the children came out for recess. When a principal of a Kauai school found his charges with their teachers outside the building during class hours, the teachers said that a child had seen a Menehune and that they were having a thorough search made for the little person. Honolulu parents find it no uncommon experience to hear their children insist that there are Menehune. And why not, if there is a Santa Claus? Menehune, goats, and tidal waves were named as some of the things feared by school children on the Waialua plantation near Honolulu in a study made by Gwladys Hughes (38).

While some children have come to fear the Menehune because parents, in the absence of a Menehune Protective Association, have used Menehune as bogeymen, other children who claim to have met a Menehune suffer only from over-excitement and retrospective fascination. The Menehune they claim to have met were friendly to them and did not harm them.

A Honolulu high school senior of Japanese descent who was interviewed for a newspaper after winning a contest told the reporter that while she was not quite sure that there really were Menehune she thought that somehow the Menehune brought her luck. She had heard that the little people brought luck, and two months before she won the contest her brother and sister with three of their friends saw a Menehune under the family house. This happened in a lane in the neighborhood of North Vineyard and North Kukui Streets. The Hawaii Visitors Bureau may check old newspapers for the correct address in case they wish to put up a "Warrior" marker there. This Menehune, who was four to five inches tall, boldly walked out from under the house into the lane and invited the children to follow him, calling in English, "Hey, fellas!" The children saw him walk right under the legs of a man reading a comic book and then he passed a child with its mother. The two adults did not see the Menehune, and the implication is that adults cannot see them. The strolling Menehune finally disappeared into Foster Gardens, from whence he was thought to have come. Although the children had fun following the Menehune, they were overcome at dusk with excitement and fear and for a week were nervous.

No connection had been suggested between the Menehune and flying saucers at the time this article was written.

Written information about the Hawaiian Menehune belongs only to the last century. It represents what has been believed about them in the years since Europeans arrived in the islands. Evidence shows that these beliefs have been changing even within the memory of living individuals and that they continue to change. By studying the kind and content of the changes occurring today in the Menehune tradition, we can infer what may have happened in the early period for which we have no documentary evidence. We can catch change on the wing, so to speak. Though change today is probably more rapid than in early times, folklorists assume that some of the same processes operate now as in the past. That is why the collecting of the versions of beliefs and myths as they exist now is important.

USE OF THE TERM MENEHUNE

The term Menehune and its dialectical variants in Polynesia have not been standardized in English usage. Every possible variation occurs, a familiar problem in the use of non-English names. In popular accounts the name is Anglicized by adding *s* to form the plural; but except in direct quotations, I have followed Rice (52, pp. 33-46), Beckwith (5, pp. 321-326), and Buck (15, pp. 475, 516), treating the word as a compound noun. The context of the sentence makes it clear whether the singular or plural is meant.

DESCRIPTION OF THE HAWAIIAN MENEHUNE AND THEIR CULTURE

PHYSICAL ANTHROPOLOGY

Material relating to the physical anthropology of the Menehune leaves much to be desired, because people who profess to have seen Menehune tend to be incoherent and because no Menehune skeletons have been submitted to anthropologists for study. Although Bishop Museum has thousands of ancient Hawaiian skeletons awaiting analysis, no preliminary survey by physical anthropologists has as yet spotted what might be a Menehune skeleton among the bones.

However, one may choose from a number of descriptions. One account has it that Menehune average two to three feet in height (Rice, 52, p. 136). Another makes them even shorter, below the knees of Naipualehu, a Kauai dwarf (apparently non-mythical and non-Menehune) who was about three feet tall (Kaiwi, 42; Thrum, 68, p. 214). The one seen in Honolulu recently, it will be recalled, was only four or five inches tall. Perhaps the word mites should be added to such informal and unscientific classifications as dwarfs, trolls, pixies, elves, gnomes, fairies, pygmies, diminutives, and little men.

Although there are women and children among the Menehune, little is said about them. No one ever claims to have seen a female Menehune. One can only wonder why. Their height in comparison with that of the men has not been reported. Analike, one of the few Menehune females ever mentioned in stories, was a girl who lived on an island that floated about the Pacific and who is described as beautiful and very petite. This is sufficient and suitable for a story description, if not for science. She married a castaway chief Keaweahu of Kona, Hawaii, who presumably was of normal size. One cannot discuss the genetics of this miscegenation because the height of their son is not given. (See Lydgate, 46, p. 135.)

The most detailed description of Menehune is that of J. H. Kaiwi (42; Thrum, 68, pp. 214-219), whose grandparents claimed to have met some Menehune while gathering sandalwood in the mountain forests of Kauai. Kaiwi describes the Menehune as having short, hairy bodies, which are stout, round, muscular, and very strong. Set in a red-skinned face are big eyes hidden by long eyebrows. A low, protruding forehead is covered with hair of undescribed color and texture. The nose is short and thick. Kaiwi adds the information that the Menehune have a set expression that makes them unpleasant to look at and inspires fear, though they are neither angry nor quarrelsome, but are good people who molest no one without cause.

J. A. Akina, Rice's informant (52), confirms that they are small, broad, and muscular with tremendous energy and strength. Thrum (62, p. 144), contrary to Kaiwi, says that Menehune are smooth-skinned with little body hair (glabrous).

Only once have the Menehune been described as a large rather than a small people. This account, which Fornander states is based on the writings of Kepelino and Kamakau, native Hawaiian historians, differs in many respects from other accounts and will be discussed later. It is sufficient to note here that the Menehune therein described are called a large, numerous, and powerful people (Fornander, 27, vol. 6, pt. 2, pp. 270-271). Though Solomon K. Kaulilili, in a manuscript in Bishop Museum, refers to the Menehune as "a large race of people," the adjective is ambiguous. Is "large" used in the sense of numerous, or is it a description of the size of the people? The entire account follows:

> The things pertaining to this race of people [the Menehune] are very strange, because in the legends concerning them and their deeds, it is mystifying.
> This was a large race of people who dwelt on the twelve islands of Hawaii in times past.
> The names of these people, formerly, was not known but later it was known that the name was Menehune because there were so many of them like the menehune shrimps in the sea.
> People guessed that these people belonged to the assembly of gods or the four thousand gods or the four hundred thousand gods.
> They made the walls of ponds and heiaus at night. These handcrafts of theirs was done in very short time. They did not work in the day time.
> On the edge of the cliff at Kalaupapa, that is at Kukui-o-Hapuu, they made a heiau with long alā stones. It is beautiful to behold.
> Please pardon me for my incorrect explanation. Your son that is poor in thought like an ant and C[?].

DEMOGRAPHY

Impressive figures have been advanced on the former population of Menehune. There is a reference to their numbers in a story published in the *Hawaii*

Holomua, April 24, 1912, of which the original news story and the translation are in Bishop Museum. The complete translation, by M. K. Pukui, is given a little later. Somewhat as in Kaulilili's account, this story states that the words used to express the numbers of Kauai Menehune were *lau* (400), *mano* (4,000), *kini* (40,000) and *lehu* (400,000), their total number being *melehuka* (millions). In this article, the Menehune are spoken of as gods. In the old days the grown men among the Kauai Menehune were so numerous that they could have formed two rows reaching from Makaweli to Wailua, a distance of about 25 miles (Rice, 52, p. 34). Once when all the Menehune of Kauai assembled they numbered more than 500,600, not counting the children under 17. The occasion of this great gathering was to prepare for their exodus from the Hawaiian Islands at the order of the king of the Menehune who was worried because so many of his men were marrying Hawaiian women and he wanted to keep the race pure. The 320,000 men made up 20 divisions, each division with 16,000 in it; the 160,000 women formed eight divisions of 20,000 each; and there were 10,000 adolescent boys, and 10,600 girls up to the age of 17. These divisions included all the active workers (Rice, 52, pp. 40-41).

Kauai consists of about 555 square miles, and the population on July 1, 1948, as estimated by the Bureau of Health Statistics, Board of Health, was 36,493.[2] In their heyday, then, before the exodus, the Menehune were extremely prolific in contrast to the present population, and Kauai was densely populated. Using only the figure 500,600 and not attempting to estimate the number of children belonging to the 160,000 mature women, I find that there were nearly 902 Menehune per square mile on the island of Kauai at the peak of the Menehune period as contrasted with the 65.7 people per square mile in 1948. This is a world record, for 902 people per square mile, with uncounted children under foot, is surpassed today probably only by modern Java, that population warren of the world. But, of course, the Menehune, being small, would not seem to be as crowded as the Malays. However, besides the Menehune on the island, stories narrate that there were also Hawaiians and the Mu, a people similar to the Menehune. (See map, figure 1.)

The sociological problems implicit in the disproportion of men to women among the Kauai Menehune are thought-provoking. There were twice as many men as women, judging from the above figures, though the proportion of adolescent boys to girls was nearly equal; there were only 600 more girls than boys. Of course, in a population of over 500,000, the problem of 600 girls without boy friends does not loom large in the total picture; but it is a little sad, particularly as one can guess that the more popular girls indulged in cut-throat competition and had more than their statistical share of escorts. Perhaps the cut-throat competition was literal. Otherwise, how can one explain why there

---

[2] Since this was written, the 1950 census credits Kauai County with 29,838 people.

were eventually twice as many adult men as women? Why did so many adult women, and presumably so many girls in their late adolescence, die? At any rate, the men, finding no mates among their own people, married Hawaiian women. This, as we have seen, the Menehune king disapproved, so on the night of a full moon, he called the men and their first-born sons together and told them that on the next night all the Menehune would leave the islands so that their racial purity could be maintained. The Menehune men were not permitted to take their Hawaiian spouses or their younger children with them. Although one man, Mohikia, protested and offered to send his son in his place, he was scolded for putting a woman, only lately come into his life, before his king. To appease the Hawaiian women and to prevent criticism of the Menehune, the newly ripened crops were left for them to harvest.

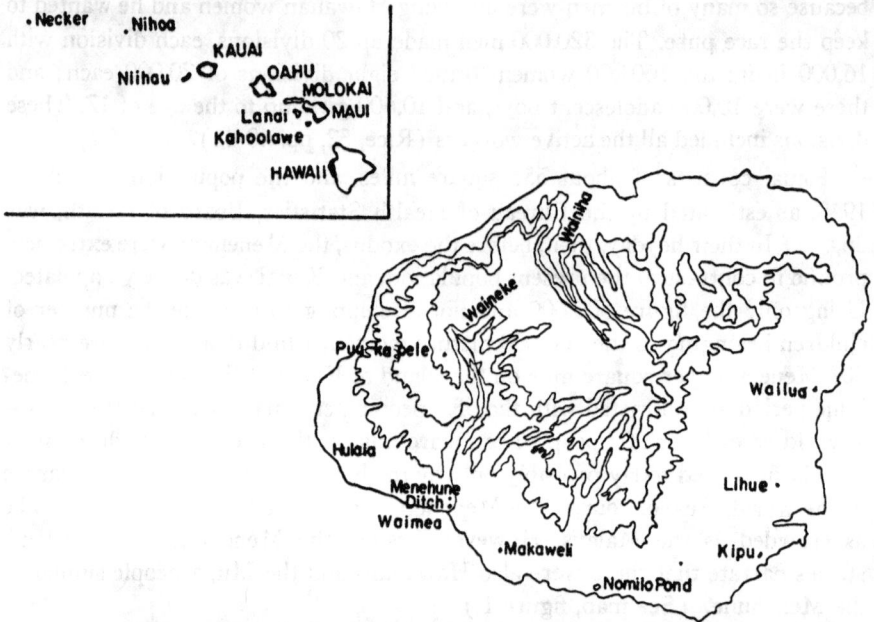

FIGURE 1.—Island of Kauai, with inset map of the Hawaiian Islands.

Apparently, however, not all the Menehune left at the time of the exodus. Perhaps a few who felt as Mohikia did hid in the forests in order to remain with their Hawaiian families, for in the reign of Kaumualii, the last independent ruler of Kauai, a census was taken of the population of Wainiha Valley in which 65 of the 2,000 people counted by the king's agent were Menehune. All 65 lived in a community named Laau (Forest) in the depths of the valley forests. This was more than 125 years ago, for Kaumualii died in 1824. As will be discussed later, it is possible that the little people counted in the census belonged to a related tribe of dwarfs rather than to the Menehune (Lydgate, 44, p. 125). A loose estimate for 1823 gives Kauai a population of 10,000, which is 20,000 less than Captain Cook estimated, or probably overestimated, in 1779 (Bennett, 6, p. 9). One wonders what the results of the 1950 census by the United States Government will reveal as to Menehune population and whether a Menehune Protective Association will formally protest the negligence of census takers if not one Menehune is counted.

No storyteller has produced census figures for the other islands, but there were always enough Menehune on any Hawaiian island to make a good story and to provide sufficient labor for any stonework required. For instance, Hawaii had enough Menehune to line up side by side for a distance of 12 miles from Pololu Valley to Honoipu, Kohala, build the Mookini Heiau in one night, and be completely finished by cock crow at dawn (Thrum, 62, p. 117). Note that these informal censuses are in terms of queueing up—singly, as on Hawaii, or doubly, as on Kauai. No storyteller, however, gives the number of Menehune per mile. To make such an estimate, several factors must be considered. For instance, their stockiness has to be balanced against their shortness. We know that most Menehune are two to three feet tall, but we do not know how wide an average, mature, male Menehune is. Rice merely says that they are a squat people. On the other hand, though Menehune are shy and difficult to catch for a count, they do line up at night to pass stones from hand to hand from the site of a quarry to the temple they are building.

Fornander (26, vol. 2, p. 36), who does not credit the Menehune with having built the Mookini Heiau, states that according to tradition, the stones for Mookini Heiau were passed hand to hand for nine miles, "a feat requiring at least some fifteen thousand working men at three feet apart." He is, presumably, speaking of normal-sized workers and not of Menehune. Being Hawaiian, these workers must have been heavy-set men, and certainly more Menehune than normal-sized men would have been required, unless one assumes that their phenomenal strength enabled them to toss the stones down the nine-mile line to Mookini. Anyway, one would have to estimate that there were far more than 15,000 Menehune men on Hawaii, let alone their families, if one were to believe that they and not the Hawaiians built this heiau. The parallelogram-shaped Mookini Heiau was 286 feet on one side, 277 feet on the other, 136 feet on one of the two shorter sides and 118 feet on the other. The walls, Fornander writes (26, vol. 2, p. 36), were more than 20 feet high and fully eight feet wide on the top. The Menehune surely had a busy evening. Traditions do not mention the wage rate, but the Menehune never had to be paid overtime, since they either finished a job in one night or left it uncompleted.

While Hawaii may have had over 15,000 of these mythical men and Kauai, over 500,000 men and women, no information is available to estimate how many Menehune formerly lived on Oahu.

PERSONALITY STRUCTURE

In recent years, anthropologists have been much concerned with the personality, or character, structure of the tribes they study. Fortunately, documentation on Menehune personality structure exists, though intensive studies of individual personalities are lacking. The information will be presented without any attempt to classify the Menehune according to the theories of the various schools of psychology. It is impossible to resist the temptation, however, to point out that as between the so-called anal and oral types of personality, the Menehune are pretty clearly of the oral, or extrovert, type in their behavior among themselves. This is rather surprising as, off hand, their seclusive, nocturnal work habits due to a dislike for being seen loom so large in popular discussion of their personalities that they seem to the casual student to be definitely introvert. I hereby submit the available data to psychologists for their final word. It is regrettable that no Rohrschach tests have been made on the Menehune, though perhaps their ability to construct heiaus and wander about at night without getting lost will serve as a substitute for the Porteus maze test.

Let us first consider them in their lighter moments, off duty. They play as hard as they work and have a reputation for being noisy chatterboxes among themselves. The hum and noise of their voices can sometimes be heard, according to one of Thrum's informants, Moke Manu, who adds, however, that the Menehune are invisible to all but their own descendants or to people connected with them (Thrum, 62, p. 113). According to Kaiwi (42, p. 115), they are a merry and talkative people with loud-voiced laughter, and their conversation sounds like the "low growl of a dog."

On three joyful occasions (Rice, 52, pp. 36, 39, 45; and Thrum, 62, p. 114), the Kauai Menehune made so much noise that they frightened the birds on Oahu. The first occasion was when their employer gave them a feast after they had finished building a dam and a watercourse. When each received one shrimp, they made such a happy racket that a saying originated, "The hum of the voices of the Menehunes at Puukapele, Kauai, startled the birds of the pond of Kawainui, at Koolaupoko, Oahu." The Kawainui birds were frightened a second time when the Menehune let out a great shout after putting a stone, a transformed Menehune, into place. The third time the birds were frightened was when the Menehune shouted at their play, as they rolled down a ten-foot hill called Popopii, which they had built on top of Kilohana, Kauai.

Fish also have been frightened by Menehune parties. Before leaving Kauai, the commoners among the Menehune built themselves a monument at the order of the king. When it was ready, their riotous celebration caused the fish in the pond of Nomilo across the island to jump in fright; and the *moi,* a wary type of fish, left the beaches (Rice, 52, p. 41).

The Oahu Menehune were as noisy and merry-hearted as their Kauai relatives (Westervelt, 71, pp. 142, 149-150). Their master, Ku-leo-nui, Ku-of-the-loud-voice, could be heard all over the island when he called them in the evening. They shouted with joy, it is said, when the owner of a canoe they had built returned safely home. Later, however, their noisiness had unhappy consequences when two supernatural beings brought from Hawaii to Oahu two magical trees to provide an unending supply of cooked food and fish. They ordered silence until the trees were settled. But the Menehune and their equally little friends of the forest, the Eepa, shouted with a great voice, for they were frightened thinking that the island was being invaded. One tree fell near Kawainui and thus failed to reach its destination in Nuuanu Valley, where it would have been a truly marvelous timesaver, a delicatessen supplying an easy source of cooked fish and other food. The god Kane was ordered by the angry and disappointed chief to drive the Menehune and the Eepa from their Waolani home in Nuuanu. No one knows where they went.

The Menehune are playful, love jokes, and have many different kinds of games. On Kauai, before the exodus, they used to carry stones from the mountains to their bathing places, throw them into the sea, and dive after them. They also liked to dive into the sea from cliffs. Rice names five or more of their Kauai bathing places (52, pp. 37-38). The game of rolling down hill has been mentioned. One of the divisions organized for the exodus from Kauai was made up of musicians, fun-makers, storytellers, and minstrels to entertain the king. Musicians used bamboo nose flutes, ti-leaf trumpets, mouth harps, and hollow log drums (52, pp. 41-42). During the exodus, when two chiefesses, Hanakapiai and Hanakeao, died, the former in childbirth and the latter in an accident, the king ordered 60 days of mourning. These were concluded with feasting and games. Among the many sports were top spinning; dart throwing, using a spear-throwing device; hiding a pebble; boxing; wrestling, both standing up and lying down; tug of war; foot racing; sled racing by both men and women down grassy slopes; and "a game resembling discus throwing." The two greatest foot racers were "so swift that they could run around Kauai six times in one day" (52, pp. 42-44), and Kauai is about 95 miles in circumference. The names of some of the outstanding performers are still remembered.

On the whole, the Menehune are plucky. The Kauai Menehune were not afraid to attack sharks and the record mentions their killing one, an event which they memorialized by erecting a pile of stones (52, p. 37). Owls and dogs, however, seem to make them nervous, perhaps because, like the Menehune themselves, owls and dogs wander about at night. The Kailioopaia Heiau on Kauai was left unfinished because first a large owl (The Owl of Kane) and then a large dog (Ku-ilio-loa), both supernatural beings, frightened the lone workman, who regarded them as evil omens and abandoned the heiau which he was building (Rice, 52, p. 38). In Manoa Valley, Oahu, once a favorite Mene-hune district, the Menehune were driven away by an owl king who was aided in his war with the Menehune by owls imported from Kauai (Westervelt, 72, pp. 131-132). According to a different and less imaginative version, Ku, an Oahu chief, forced the Menehune to leave upper Manoa Valley, where they had built the Kukaoo Heiau and, across the road from it, Ulumalu Fort (Thrum, 61, p. 112; 65, pp. 45, 60).

In general, the Menehune are kind and helpful to other people, especially to their descendants (Thrum, 62, p. 114). They work for others when asked, or even when not asked. For instance, after residents of Pepeekeo, near Hilo, Hawaii, had assembled rocks to build a heiau, the Menehune surprised them by building the heiau in one night before the people got around to putting the rocks into place (62, p. 117). They also befriended Eternal Fire, a little Hawai-ian girl who had been abandoned by her parents and adopted by a poor couple. They let her pick sacred mountain plants, and when the Hawaiian king's over-seer fell in love with her, they prepared a dowry for her (Green, 31, pp. 70-79).

They built for the hero Laka (not the divine patroness of the hula) a canoe so that he could go in search of his lost father. Laka first tried to do the work himself. He cut down a suitable tree, but the next morning found it upright with every twig in place. After this had happened several times, he dug a hole under the fallen tree to spy on the people conspiring against him. When he heard the noise of talking and chanting, he caught two little men who agreed to build him a canoe if he would spare them and provide them with a canoe shed and food. When the canoe was ready, the Menehune, for it appears they were the workmen, lifted the heavy canoe and started Laka on his journey (Thrum, 62, pp. 115-116). Menehune also kindly built canoes for Kakae and Kahanai, two Oahu chiefs who wished to seek lost relatives (Thrum, 66, p. 31; Wester-velt, 71, pp. 141-142).

If the Menehune are offended by anyone, they turn the offender to stone. According to Rice (52, p. 36), they regard thievery with contempt and mete out death to the culprits by transforming them into stone. They once turned some Kauai Hawaiians to stone for trying to steal from their gardens. And a Menehune watermelon thief was also turned to stone. Boastful and malingering Menehune workmen were also punished in this way.

Menehune are intelligent, industrious, conscientious, obedient to their leaders, well-organized, highly specialized in their work, and highly disciplined (Rice, 52, pp. 34-35). They are united in their work and, in general, are in perfect agreement in their way of living and working (Thrum, 62, pp. 112-117; Kaiwi, 42, pp. 114-118). Their industry has originated a byword, "No task is difficult. It is the work of one hand." The same story in which this saying occurs narrates that when the Eepa were late in bringing a canoe they had been assigned to make, they met the Menehune who were already on their way home after launching their canoe at the mouth of Nuuanu River in Honolulu (Westervelt, 71, pp. 141-142).

Menehune unity was procured by stern measures, for the men worked under strict discipline maintained by overseers, as shown by several examples (Rice, 52, pp. 36-42; Thrum, 67, p. 144). One worker who left a group of fishermen to visit a Hawaiian family escaped being transformed into a stone only because his discovery of a fresh-water spring pleased his compatriots. Another, a stone carver who ran out on his job (up a steep cliff), was turned to stone. And a boaster who said he could catch the legs of the moon failed and was turned to stone. The names of some of the overseers are still known (Rice, 52, p. 36; Thrum, 67, p. 144). Laka's canoe was under the supervision of the overseers, Mokuhalii and Kapaaikee. Papaenaena was the overseer who directed the building of the Kauai watercourse, a major Menehune job, and he, or someone of the same name, was also the chief fisherman. However, as discussed earlier, Menehune are a happy people despite the rigidity of their discipline.

The Oahu Menehune of Nuuanu and Waolani did not always agree. Pohaku-a-Umeume is a stone, 10 feet long and four and a half feet high, edged with many small cavities made by the clutching fingers of the Nuuanu and the Waolani Menehune who struggled for possession of the rock. The Waolani Menehune won the stone, which is now located near the Oahu Country Club (McAllister, 47, p. 86).

Warfare either among the Menehune or with other people in Nuuanu Valley led two Menehune to leave Nuuanu for Kalihi Valley, where they became two pointed, four-foot-high stones, one on each side of the stream near the head of the valley. Strangers in the territory must lay a wreath on the stones if they want good weather on their trip to Kilohana and back. If they fail, the Menehune will sprinkle water from a leaf of a tree fern or a branch of the flowering mountain apple onto the stones to cause the summit of Kapo to be covered with mist and a drenching rain. But the capricious Menehune sometimes throw away the wreaths and make rain anyway (McAllister, 47, p. 89).

To summarize, Menehune fear daylight and avoid being seen, and they work only at night. Every job must be finished by dawn, or it is left. There is a saying, "In one night, and by dawn it is finished." Only four incomplete jobs are known: a Kauai heiau mentioned earlier, a Kauai fishpond, the transporting of Kakae's canoe to the ocean, and a watercourse on Hawaii (Rice, 52, p. 36; Thrum, 66, p. 31; 62, p. 114; 70, p. 86; and Kaiwi, 42, p. 115). The heiau was left unfinished because an owl and a dog were regarded as evil omens. The others were left unfinished because daylight came before the work was done.

HOUSING, DIET, AND ECONOMY

Menehune culture is simple. The people live in banana-leaf huts (Kaiwi, 42), or in hidden caves or hollow logs. Rice reports that the head fisherman had a home hollowed out of a stone (52, pp. 35, 36). Before leaving Kauai, they had neither fire nor cooked food, but pounded their raw food on stones, some of which are still to be seen (Rice, 52, p. 36). However, when the Hawaiian chief married Analike, the Menehune girl who lived on the floating island, he taught the people to make fire and to prepare cooked food (Lydgate, 46). Contrarily, part of the Menehune dowry for the orphan girl, Eternal Fire, included cooked food (Green, 31, pp. 70-79).

Opinions about Menehune diet also differ slightly. One story about Analike, in which she is described as the god Kane's eldest daughter, tells of her marriage to a Hawaiian chief who ate what she considered rat food—bananas and sugar cane—whereas she ate berries (Green, 31; Rice, 52, pp. 19-31). One authority states that Menehune do not eat bananas or other wild fruit, as people provide them with food (Thrum, 67, p. 144). According to another, they eat wild vegetable food but supplement it with what they earn for their stonework, usually shrimp. One or two bananas and a single handful of shrimp or silversides are enough to satisfy Menehune hunger (Kaiwi, 42). According to a third authority, Menehune like arrowroot, squash, and sweet potatoes, in addition to shrimp, greens, and an occasional ulua (a kind of fish) (Rice, 52, p. 35).

Menehune economy appears to be based largely on what they earn working for other people. Wages are low. It is a great day when an employer provides enough shrimp so that each Menehune gets one all to himself (Thrum, 62, 64, 1909). Much of their work appears to be done for nothing, from the goodness of their hearts. Although the Menehune are generally regarded as artisans employed by chiefs, Rice (52, p. 45) only once mentions their actually being employed, by Chief Ola who gave them a feast when they finished the Kauai dam and watercourse. According to Kaiwi (42, p. 115), the Menehune sometimes suffer food shortages. One such famine was between jobs, after they had finished Ola's work and before they had been employed to build two fishponds for a Hawaiian chief and his sister. Rice (52, p. 35), however, says that Menehune always have sufficient food, because they work hard at cultivating. He adds that they do not take food from other lands. Perhaps this statement is an indirect answer to those who call them thieves.

Actually, it is doubtful whether the Menehune are farmers. Only Rice mentions them as cultivators, who plant wild taro, ferns, breadfruit, bananas, and yams (52, pp. 35, 38, 40, 42, 46).

Menehune have some skill in the domestic arts, for they provided Eternal Fire with carved wooden bowls, an item also mentioned by Rice as of Menehune manufacture.

No one describes what a Menehune man, woman, or child wears, if anything. The red stocking caps and long white beards worn by the Menehune on Hawaii Visitors Bureau maps are apparently inspired by Scandinavian trolls.

STONEWORK

It is as stoneworkers that the Menehune excel. They have built heiaus, watercourses, fishponds, causeways, rock piles, and stone canoes; rearranged boulders; dug caves; and made many forest roads and trails. The Kauai dam and watercourse, the so-called "Menehune Ditch"—a job of fitted and dressed stone work and engineering which involved turning the course of Waimea River and directing the water around a corner of a mountain—still commands respect (Bennett, 6). A watercourse at Kohala, Hawaii, was left unfinished when a cock crowed and daylight came (Thrum, 70, p. 86). Both Kauai and Molokai Islands have Menehune fishponds (Rice, 52, p. 36; Fornander, 26, vol. 2, p. 6). Stone canoes dug out by Menehune are found on Kauai, and innumerable odd rock piles and individual rocks are associated with the Menehune, with each rock named (Rice, 52). Also, ruins of staunch wooden canoes abandoned by the Menehune were once to be seen on Kauai and Oahu (Rice, 52, pp. 36, 45; Thrum, 70, p. 86).

There is a saying for which I am unable to supply a scientific reference, as I saw it on a calendar years ago, "Happy is the man whose work is his hobby." The Menehune must be happy, as they love their work. They carry rocks from the seashore to the mountain sides to build heiaus or watercourses as part of their daily, or rather nightly, work; and they spend their leisure hours carrying rocks from the mountains to the seashore, so that they can either dive off the rocks or throw them into the water and dive after them.

Although the Menehune prefer to live in deep forests in remote valleys and on mountainsides, evidences of their work are scattered widely, especially on Kauai and Oahu with which they are very closely connected. Rice (52, pp. 35-48) names many celebrated Menehune sites on Kauai, although Kaiwi says (42, p. 114) that Waineke was their favorite district. Manoa and Nuuanu Valleys and the slopes of Punchbowl are Menehune centers of residence on Oahu.

Heiaus said to have been built by the Menehune are of particular value in studying the growth of Menehune traditions. Thrum, on the basis of his own study of Hawaiian temples and a review of early records including those of the Hawaiian historian, Kamakau, names 23 heiaus that are credited to the Menehune. They are found on Oahu, Kauai, Maui, Molokai, Hawaii, and even on small Niihau. Emory, Rice, Fornander, and the author of an unsigned manuscript in Bishop Museum, dated 1885, mention some not included in Thrum's list, bringing the total to 34. There are 10 on Oahu; six on Maui; three on

Hawaii; one on Niihau; four on Molokai; and 10 on Kauai. The references are not always clear as to whether a certain name applies to the heiau itself or to the place near which its ruins are found.

Thrum (61, p. 112; 62, p. 117; 64, 1907, pp. 54, 56, 60; 69, pp. 30-32; 65, 1907, pp. 40, 44, 45, 48; 70, p. 86) identifies six Oahu heiaus as being of Menehune construction: Kaheiki, Mauoki, Upo (that is, Ulupo), Kapukapuakea, Puu-o-Mahuka (which is the largest heiau on Oahu), and Kukaoo. Kapukapuakea was of wood, not of stone like the others. Kukaoo in Manoa Valley is the only heiau which the Menehune are said to have built for their own use. They lost it and the valley to the owls, according to a tradition mentioned earlier; another, more matter-of-fact, version states that a historical chief named Ku drove them out in 1700 and rebuilt the temple. Fornander (26, vol. 2, p. 23) names six Menehune-built heiaus on Oahu: Kaheiki [also on Thrum's list], Mauiki [Mauoki?], Kawaewae, Eku, Kamoalii, and Kuaokala. For Oahu, this makes 10 heiaus credited to Menehune workmen, if Mauiki and Mauoki are different, which I doubt.

On Maui in 1910, Thrum (69, p. 27; 70, p. 86) learned that three heiaus of Menehune construction were Haleokane, Puukini, and Pihana; and Kenneth Emory tells me that in 1921, when he made an archeological survey of Maui, the largest heiau on the island, Loaloa at Kaupo, was credited to the Menehune by the Hawaiians, although 10 years earlier it was recalled that King Kekaulike had built it in 1730. Fornander (26, vol. 2, p. 133) also mentions Kekaulike as the builder. However, according to a manuscript dated 1885 and stored in Bishop Museum, Menehune were the builders. The history of other heiaus near Loaloa had also been forgotten in 1921, but I do not know who is now credited with building them. Two other heiaus described in the 1885 manuscript as being of Menehune construction are Popoiwi and Momoku.

On Hawaii, Thrum found three heiaus said to be of Menehune origin: Mookini, Napule, and one at Pepeekeo (62, p. 117; 70, p. 86). Niihau had only Kihawahine (Rice, 52, p. 35; Thrum, 70, p. 86). On Molokai were Pakui, Moaula, Waikolu, and Iliiliopoi, the latter the principal heiau on the island and a college for priests (Thrum, 61, p. 117; 65, 1909, p. 40; 64, 1909, p. 50; 70, p. 86), perhaps the same heiau that Fornander (26, vol. 2, pp. 91, 102) calls Iliiliopae but does not credit to Menehune.

Thrum names six heiaus of Menehune construction on Kauai: Polihale, Kapaula, Elekuni or Elekuna (of wood, not stone), Malae, Poliahu, and Kailioahaia (65, 1907, p. 40; 69, p. 34; 70, p. 86). Rice (52, pp. 35, 37, 38, 46) does not mention Kailioahaia but adds four others, which, so far as I can identify them, are not listed by Thrum. Kailioopaia was the one left unfinished because the owl and the dog frightened the Menehune workmen. Hauola was built for Chief Ola. Other Menehune heiaus, according to Rice, were at Kalalau and Homaikawaa.

As for stories that Menehune transported stones 10 or more miles for their structures, Bennett (6, p. 40) explains how unreliable the accounts are.

There is considerable mythological and some traditional evidence that the stones for building heiaus were carried great distances. Rice . . . records the legends that the heiaus of Elekuna, Polihale, Kapa-ula, Male and Poliahu were all built by the Menehunes with stones brought from Makaweli. The archaeological evidence, however, does not substantiate these beliefs. Although some of the stones of a famous temple might have been taken to be built into a new temple, a practice recorded for other parts of Polynesia, especially Tahiti, most of the heiaus were constructed from the stones in their immediate vicinity. In fact no heiau examined was constructed of stones foreign to its locality. This means that the type of construction is limited to the materials at hand.

Below is the complete story, mentioned earlier, translated into English from the *Hawaii Holomua*. It is called a legend (*moolelo*) about Pi, who figures in other Menehune stories.

There was a certain man named Pi who was related to the strange-bodied beings called Melehune or Menehune. The words used to express their numbers in Hawaiian were *lau* (400), *mano* (4,000), *kini* (40,000), and *lehu* (400,000) of their gods. Their total number was *melehuka* (millions).

Pi was living at Hulaia on Kauai when the chief of that place began a large bank for a taro patch which was called Alakoko, to separate it from the river. This chief and his people had worked hard for some time but the task was far from being finished. The chief had paid much to the men in food, fish, tapas, and loin cloths. These were the payments agreed upon by the men for that hard work that darkened their backs in the sun.

While they worked at their hard and difficult task, Pi did not take part, but spent his time sleeping. That was his favorite occupation every day, and he was called a lazy fellow. Every evening the workers came home with the reward agreed upon, and their wives and children had food. Pi's children saw the worker's children eating fish and they cried aloud to their mother, teasing her for fish. Theirs was the only house that was without fish, for Pi wasn't given any because he was lazy and did not go to work. His wife thought it over and felt ashamed for her children and pity for their crying, so she said to Pi, "Why do you always sleep? Are you not ashamed of the crying of your children as they beg the others for fish? Go to work that our children may have life."

The next morning Pi awoke and went to the upland to cook taro. He made as many bundles of food as there were Menehune (literally, peculiar gods) he wanted to see. For each one a bundle large enough to satisfy his hunger. This was the first time that Pi had ever done any work. He pulled up a large kukui tree and put the food up on this branch and on that. Then he carried them to the lowland. That night, he carried the tree and the food he had placed on them to the place where the chief's work was. This was for his relatives, the Menehune.

They did the work just as those who made *o'opu* fish dams did at the streams, standing in a row from the place where the digging was done to the place where the closing was to be. So did the Menehune work, the first took up a stone, handed it to the one standing beside him and so on. The night had not turned into day when the task was completed by Pi and his fellow gods.

After the work was done, they made ready to eat but there was nothing to eat with their poi. They did not care for any fish that was divided up, but the multitude of shrimps in the streams supplied each one.

The next day the chief and his men came to work but they found it done. They guessed that Pi and his gods did the work, so the chief sent one of his overseers to ask. The overseer found that it was indeed he that did it. The chief sent a large number of men to carry quantities of fish and bundles of tapa to his house. The other men regretted their poverty and lack of gifts because Pi had finished the work, for this was how they were supplied by the chief with tapa and other things. Pi did not share with them because they never gave him anything before.

Olo [Ola], Waimea's high chief, heard of the finishing of the work by Pi in a single night, so he sent for him to come to Kikiaola Point so that there would be water at Peekauai. He and his men were working on it but they had not finished it.

Pi went to do it and finished it in a single night as he did before. It was a fixed custom with the Menehune to finish a piece of work in one night. It was said that these were small people who worked unitedly. If a visitor should go to Kauai, he can see this wonderful ditch made by the Menehune.

The tale is ended.

Akina, Rice's informant (52), gives slightly different information about the building of the Menehune Ditch and the Alakoko fishpond. He narrates that when Chief Ola was born the Menehune who were in New Zealand returned to Kauai at the request of Ola's father, the Waimea chief, who sent his overseer to get the little people who were not gods, as stated above, but merely supernormally strong. It was after their return that they "built the wall of the Alakoko fish pond at Niumalu. Standing in two rows they passed the stones from hand to hand all the way from Makaweli to Niumalu. Daylight came before they had finished the work, and two gaps were left in the wall. These were filled in by Chinamen in late years, and the pond is still in use."

While Pi is not mentioned in Akina's account above, he does appear in the story of the building of the Menehune Ditch, as Ola's magician, or kahuna. Ola, a good king, wanted to help his people who had trouble bringing water from Waimea River to their taro patches on the flats. Pi advised Ola to "establish a *kapu* so that no one can go out of his house at night. Then I shall summon the Menehune to build a stone water-lead around the point of the Waimea River so that your people will always have an abundant water supply."

The tapu established, all the people stayed in their houses, the chickens were shut in calabashes, and the dogs were muzzled, so that there was absolute silence on the night when the Menehune were to work. "Then Pi summoned the Menehune to come from foreign lands and make the water-lead in one night. Beforehand Pi had arranged the stones in a cliff, every one of the same size and shape. From this cliff each Menehune took one stone which he called Haawe-a-Pi, the Pack-of-Pi, and placed it in the lead." The watercourse they built is still called Kiki-a-Ola, Ola's-water-lead, and parts of it are still visible. It represents one of the few examples of dressed stone work in the Hawaiian Islands.

It was after they finished this task that a feast was given the Menehune at the Hauola Heiau, where they made so much noise that they frightened the birds on Oahu.

Thrum (62) also connects Pi with the Menehune, as their supervisor. Pi, he writes, was an ordinary man of Waimea, Kauai, who got the Menehune from the mountains of Puukapele to build a dam across the river and a water-course from there to a place near Kikiaola. On the night he set for the work, each Menehune carried a stone. Then Pi gave the great feast at which they made so much racket. Thrum, like Akina, states that the wall of the fishpond at the end of the Huleia River was not finished by dawn, hence was left.

Still another version (Kaiwi, 42) states that the famous watercourse was completed during the night of Akua, on which there was a full moon. The Menehune stood in line from above the head of the watercourse to below Poli-hale to pass stones, a distance of five or six miles. After they had finished, there was not enough food to maintain them so they moved away to build two fish-ponds, one for Alekoko (Alakoko, above), young chief of Puna, Kauai, and one for his sister, Ka-lala-lehua. Both lived between Kipu River and Niumalu. The brother's pond was finished, the sister's was not.

Sometimes Ola is called Kikiaola. Apparently the famous Menehune Ditch won him the name of Ola's-water-lead. A romantic story has the Menehune and the Mu, a people sometimes said to be their relatives, living on a beautiful floating island which anchors near Kauai. Hulukumanuna, a famous jumping kahuna endowed with great foresight, declared to King Kikiaola that only the Menehune could build a dam at Waimea. He received his wisdom about the Menehune from the god Kane, who told him to go to Kanehunamoku, chief of the floating island, bearing his name or that of Kueihelani, and ask for Mene-hune aid. The dam, which was begun during May (Makalii), had Papaenaena as overseer. When it was finished, King Kikiaola slept on the altar and was deluged with water, for a human sacrifice of the rank of chief was needed.

Social Organization

The social organization of the Kauai Menehune parallels that of the Hawai-ians, and the narrator of Rice's version doubtless drew upon his knowledge of old Hawaiian life in building up his account of Menehune society, as he did in describing their food and organized specialists in entertainment. They have a king, queen, chiefs, chiefesses, overseers, foremen, heralds, marshals, magicians of various kinds, entertainers, and a class of commoners. (Names of individual Menehune have been preserved.) Although discipline is strict and enforced with severe sanctions, the little people speak their minds at times, as when they gathered to plan for leaving Kauai. But the king has the last word; Mene-hune lie on their faces before him to show obedience, as was the old Hawaiian custom (Rice, 52, pp. 33-46).

The above-quoted sources are the only ones which tell us of the culture of the Menehune. However, anthropologists, professional or amateur, may feel competent, armed with this survey, to undertake expeditions to Waineke Valley, Kauai, or to Manoa Valley, Oahu, former Menehune strongholds, in search of more data about them. As in their physical anthropology, gaps in our knowledge of the social anthropology of the Menehune should certainly be filled in by careful and sober observers. However, certain complications have been evaded thus far which must now be faced and described to the prospective field worker.

RELATED TYPES OF HAWAIIAN LITTLE PEOPLE

The investigator may feel that even on a dark night he could recognize a Menehune because any tiny person seen in a secluded wooded place, perhaps loaded down with a rock, must be a Menehune. However, there are little people other than the Menehune in the Hawaiian Islands and they are not easy to distinguish. Everyone knows how hard it is to be sure of what one sees in a thick forest on a dark, lonely night when light is provided only by a flickering little fire.

Anyone who thinks he has seen a Menehune must be prepared to prove (1) that he is a relative of a Menehune, since otherwise the Menehune would not be visible to him, and (2) that it was not really a Mu, a Wa, or perhaps a Wao, rather than a Menehune. It might even have been an Eepa. Modern belief is that, all things considered, children have a better chance than adults to see a Menehune.

Identification sounds deceptively easy if the little person can be observed in side view, for "the abdomens of the Menehunes are very distended while those of the Mu's are round" (Thrum, 67, p. 144). The observer should, however, keep his head and make further observations as to whether the little person is glabrous or hairy, for the Mu are said to be bearded and hairy-bodied, whereas a Menehune might be either since opinions differ (p. 10). And there are other means of identification. If the little person is eating a banana and not carrying a rock, he is probably a Mu, for it is doubtful whether the Menehune eat or carry bananas. Kaiwi's grandparents, who had roasting bananas stolen from them by little people, admitted that the Menehune are sometimes confused with the Mu (Kaiwi, 42, p. 118). The reputation of the Menehune for honesty is rather strongly insisted upon, it will be recalled, and punishment for thievery is severe among them. Whether the Menehune eat bananas, raw or cooked, stolen or otherwise, is definitely a moot question on which defenders of the Menehune reputation are more vocal than are the members of the Mu Protective Society.

Lydgate (44; 45, pp. 25-31), the authority on the Mu, learned about them from a Hawaiian on Kauai who declared that he knew a woman who was the daughter of a Hawaiian prince and a half-Mu commoner. The half-Mu's father was a Hawaiian bird-catcher, but her mother was one of *the* Mu from Laau, the same, exclusive, forested community where Kaumualii's census taker counted 65 Menehune over a century ago. Lydgate thinks that the census taker erred; that these people really were Mu, who are even more *kama'aina* than the Menehune. Lydgate says that the Mu are "an allied race of older extraction," aborigines of the land driven into the mountains.

The Mu are brown, diminutive (about the same height as the Menehune), stocky, and active. Their heads are shaggy and their beards and eyebrows bushy. Their speech—full of strange, uncanny grunts and cries—differs from the Hawaiian. The people are wild, easily frightened, and always alert for escape, which they accomplish very quickly. They come to the lowlands to steal fish, poi, and roasting bananas, and to snatch tapas off sleepers. According to Thrum (67, p. 43), they lack fire, clothing, and domestic arts, though another account ascribes clothes of dried ti and banana leaves to them. They have banana-leaf huts and eat wild bananas from the luxuriant groves at Laau. The lauhala mats mentioned in the story of the wooing of the Mu girl by a prince belonged perhaps to her Hawaiian father and were not of Mu manufacture. The prince had a hard time catching the girl because Mu have a fine sense of smell and are fleet-footed.

Lydgate translates Mu-ai-maia, the full name of the people, as "banana planters," a literal translation is "banana-eating-bugs." There is no connection between the Banana-eating Mu and the Man-eating Mu, who were a miserable and hated group of Hawaiian men who had to find human sacrifices for the heiaus.

A Hawaiian newspaper, *Aloha Aina*, for October 24, 1893, starts an unsigned, rambling account about the Mu, the Banana Eaters of Laau-haele-mai, Kauai. For about 17 installments, which have been translated for Bishop Museum by Mary K. Pukui, the story tells about the adventures of an unnamed *kilo* (one who watches for schools of fish) of the Mu race. From the first two installments which give general information about this race, I have selected the following excerpts.

In the time of the ancient chiefs of Hawaii nei, a certain race of people lived at Wainiha on Kauai. The place where these people lived was on the southeast of the long valley just above the face of Hinanalele and Pohaku-loa. The writer guessed that from the sea at Kaumakainalehua in Luluupali to Laau is about 30 or 40 miles.

It is good land, a level one, and afforded a good living in the chilly dews of the mountain. It is about 10 or more miles from Laau to Waialeale and the area of Laau covers about 50 or 60 acres of land. Its river lies directly on the southwestern side of Mt. Waialeale to Wainiha.

These people who are unrelated to the Menehune and had no chiefs over them except He who made Mankind . . .

Many plants grew on the land of the Mu . . . The plant that grew there the most was the banana and that was the food of these mountain dwellers. They lived without a thought of chiefs, or overseers, to watch over them. This (Hawaiian) race was not like that in the olden days. The Mu were a cunning people and clever in all that they did.

The narrator then describes the culture of these people, but I shall break off and insert a section about the history of the Mu as told briefly in the story. They were kidnapped by Kalaulehua, a Kauai man, from Kanehunamoku, the chief of the famous floating island bearing his name or that of Kuaihelani [Kueihelani]. The Mu "were brought to make water flow on the eastern side of Waialeale, facing Wailua on Kauai. These people refused to do it and would not go. [They said], 'We shall stay until the day comes when we will disappear from here.' It is true that they have vanished today."

The story goes on to give the division of this people as "the Mu, the Na-mu, the Na-wa, the Heleliko, the Imihia, the Iku-ka-mu of the land of Puna where the Waikoloa blows, the wild wind from Hauola." It will be noted that the Mu are distinguished from Na-mu. Who the last three named groups of people are, I do not know.

Angry because the Mu refused to obey his orders, Kalaulehua told the kidnapped people that they could go seek their own lord, but that they must take no plants from the land which he was going to tapu. They could have land "from Pohakuloa up to Ka-ua-ikanana." He said that he would go to his side, and they could go to their side, but they must never set foot on his land. He declared that he had wasted his time bringing the Mu.

The chief had captured seven Mu, four women and three men and a *kaioe* blossom, a large, reddish-yellow flower, later to be mentioned by the exiles in their chants. Their captor made them "climb at Waikuauhoe and live at Honopu Waiakua." A sad chant commemorates the event.

> The cliffs from whence we came,
> Walking a straight trail, climbing a steep one,
> With aching knees, falling,
> Exhausted, wearied, limping,
> Looking askance, begging,
> Bold, shameless,
> A people who came where they did not belong,
> Whose roots hung exposed,
> To become a banana eating population
> Of the upland of Laau-haele-mai.
>
> O Ku-kaili-moku, Kanehunamoku,
> Ruling chief, chief of the whole island,
> Dweller of the island, roller away of the island,
> The thousands have departed from Laau-haele-mai,
> Bearing their burdens on their backs,
> Carrying their babies in their arms,
> They turned their faces toward Kuaihelani,
> The unstable land in the deep blue sea,
> The dark, blue sea of Kane.

The Mu settled in the mountain region their captor assigned them, and their numbers increased. Following is the description of their mode of life as narrated in the story.

They had homes, and this was the way they built them. They were made with thin and long sticks. Their houses were made long like a shed, covered over with dried banana leaves, ti leaves, fern leaves, and so on. When that was finished, a large fire place was built in the center of the house. They made four sleeping places. The first division sat by the fireplace and did the roasting of the bananas on either side of it. The second division ate the bananas and all other foods cooked in the fireplace. When the fireplace was re-lighted, those in front went to the back and to their turn in eating bananas. This was a fixed custom among the Mu people, for bananas were their daily food.

Their sleeping tapas were made of dried banana leaves, woven like ti leaf coverings and knotted to fibers extracted from banana stems. Their loin cloths were made of banana fibers, and the women wore ti leaves made into skirts like hula skirts.

The coverings over their sleeping places were made of dried banana leaves, and the sleeping place occupied one side of the house. The dried banana leaves were heaped up high, and when it was bed time, the men went to the center where the dried leaves were heaped and laid down. The women slept where the first division sits [by the fireplace], and the men did not go near for a sexual act. The place where they did the playing of their bodies was by the stream.

They were fast climbers of trees and rocks slippery with moss.

They were a stout, broad-shouldered, and short people who delighted in the cold. . . . It was said that these people were still living in the upland of Laau just a few years prior to the arrival of Captain Cook. It is a large mountain place and suitable for taro growing, and many taro patches can be made there. The sea is not visible for it is too far away.

The story goes on to narrate customs relating to birth. A house of dried banana leaves was built a few days before the event. A shiny *ala* stone was placed in the center of the hut. A cup of *'awa* was prepared. If the child was a boy, the midwife called out:

> O Kane-alohi of the uplands of Ka-waa-loa here!
> A loud shouter, a climber, a leaf bud,
>   a descendant of the stormy rain clouds.
> The young taro shoot grows till it touches
>   the corner of Pohakuloa!

If a girl was born she chanted:

> Growing together with the *kaioe* blossom,
> Growing closely together, a thin stripling,
> Dedicated to the work of spreading dried banana leaves,
> A carrier of bundles; one born in the arms of Hinaiaeleele,
> Set apart for the tapus of women.

When the relatives came to see the baby at the proper time to take it to the shrine, the child, if it was a boy, was wrapped in dried, split ti leaves tied to a netting of banana fibers. The wizard at the shrine, which was called Nuumea-kapu and which is said still to be there, did not touch the baby with his hands but with a long stick. If the baby was a girl, the midwife offered the prayer herself. Then ti-leaf whistles were blown, nose flutes of bamboo were sounded, and gourd whistles added to the noise which went on for two weeks.

The Mu had three heiaus, "one for success in jumping off cliffs, one for success in fish catching, and one for the sacred worship of the gods." Then there was a fish shrine for the increase of *o'opu* fish, and another for its spawn.

Mu were divided into two work divisions, "one for Pohakuloa and the second for Hinanalele." If the fish watcher for the *o'opu* failed to make offerings at the shrines or if he made a mistake, a flood would sweep the land.

The *o'opu* trap (*kahe-o'opu*) made by the Mu was very large, 10 to 20 fathoms long. While the Mu method of making the trap is probably similar to that of other ancient Kauai people, I present it below for its material culture value.

A proclamation was sent to the two divisions from one end to the other to go to the mountains to cut wood for a frame and sticks to lay across it. The head worker of these people came in the evening to see if they were ready.

Half the people went. The owner took a log of *'ohi'a lehua* to use as a support for the front of the trap. This support was called a pillow (*uluna*). It was he who had to lay it on the head of the trap. No one else was allowed there except those he wanted and selected. Five men were sufficient and they did the work without uttering a word or whispering to fellow companions until one side was completed. Then their overseer examined the work and nodded approval. They turned together to face the other side and thus they worked until the chief's, landlord's and commoner's tapu period had passed.

When the head worker saw that all was done, then the head worker above him lighted a fire to free the tapu and the rest of the people could come. At the completion of the trap, the fish-watcher and the owner performed their duties. They took a stone from the pool Kolokini Kaawakoa below Waialeale. . . . The fish-watcher went there to make his offerings of *'awa*, bananas, and *kumu* taro. When that was done he made a cup of *olona* leaves and put it on the edge of the pool of this spring and chanted.

The story then tells what happened when the magician who had set the tapu on the lands for Kalaulehua died and left only the fish-watcher as the religious man of the tribe.

Pointing out that he had special duties, just as did the midwife, and that he could not perform the magician's duties he declared that a kahuna was necessary for the growing population and he would go to the plains to seek one.

The rest of the long story narrates in great detail the wandering of the fish-watcher in the plains and his constant loneliness for the land, Kanehunamoku, from which his people had been exiled. Humor is given the story by the heat he feels from the sun as he descends, for the mountain home was cool. After acting as a very lucky fish-watcher for some of the people below who admire his skill and his chanting, he is visited by a kahuna whose secret knowledge is of the Mu's need for him. He is a relative of the Mu, and has come from the floating island to serve a Kauai chief at the request of the god Kane.

The fish-watcher has enormous strength, for he can carry in one bundle what 8 times 40,400 men can carry. He brings his share of the fish caught in the plains to his Mu relatives in the mountains who ask about the kahuna, whom he has forgotten to bring back.

So he returns to Wainiha where he acquires great wisdom. Instead of being merely a *kilo*, fish-watcher, he becomes a *kilokilo,* reader of omens. Joining the kahuna, his relative, he is treated as an honored guest. He travels on, for his goal now is to make a journey around the island. At a place inhabited by ghosts, he restores some of them to life by working over them "twice 10 days and two nights more."

Then he sees Kanehunamoku near Kaauhau Point and goes aboard the floating island, where he is recognized as a relative and given great mana. He returns to Laau to discuss with the other Mu plans for returning to the floating island. When they go aboard, all except the reader of omens, who is last aboard, are sent into quarantine to a sheltered side of the island for ritual purification before rejoining their fellow travelers on the floating island. Reader of omens plays a final joke. He gives his innocent Mu relatives 'awa to drink but tells them it is the juice of the sweet potato root. Soon "all became leaning to one side in groups of threes." Someone, not specified, who "guessed that the naughty reader of omens had made them drink 'awa, called in English, 'Pour into them a barrel of castor oil and an ounce of epsom salts to a quart of water.' So did the Mu people talk English and because of such talk, the mischievous reader of omens laughed in glee. I, too, laughed. That is the end."

As can be seen, the prolix writer has taken the opportunity to bore his readers with detailed descriptions of ancient Hawaiian customs under the pretext of describing the Mu. But the general agreement of the description of the little Mu with accounts given by others is clear. Although no relationship is seen between them and the Menehune, and the Mu are given advanced traits like farming and the use of fire, they are described as a mythical people from beautiful Kuaihelani on the "deep, blue sea, the dark, blue sea of Kane."

Who were the Wao or Nawao? The Nawao were the banana-eating bug people of Laau (*ka lahui mu ai maia o Laau haeleele*), in other words, the Mu. Mu-ai-maia apparently is an epithet describing the Wao. One reference describes them as ancestors of the Mu. Detectable is a familiar process in the growth of folklore of what started as an epithet assuming independent existence as the complete name of a newly invented being, people, or place. The Wao-mu-ai-maia become two different groups, the Wao and the Mu. The Wao were numerous once but are now extinct. The Wao and the Menehune are cousins, for they are descended from two brothers, according to Fornander's account (27, vol. 6, pt. 2, pp. 270-271, 277) said to be based on Kepelino and Kamakau. The term Wao means "forest."

Where do the Eepa belong, if at all, on this family tree? The term means "deceit" and is applied to mythological characters who act in a peculiar and irrational manner. According to one account, the Eepa are synonymous with the Namunawa, a collective term for the Mu and the Wa (*na* is an article indicating the plural), two classes of woodland spirits. The Eepa, then, are woodland spirits of two different classes, the Mu and the Wa. The Wa, so far as I know, are not listed on any genealogy and therefore constitute as great a mystery as any of these bands. The distinguishing characteristics of each class are not defined in the source material.

The Eepa, who play tricks and assume many disguises, though no published story illustrates this point, are ruled by Anuenue (Rainbow), sister of Kane and Kanaloa. They have some artisan skill, since they built Kahanai's canoe and a temple at Waolani in Nuuanu (Westervelt, 71, p. 142; Johnstone, 41, pp. 160-167).

S. M. Kamakau, a native Hawaiian historian, who wrote extensively and in a popular fashion for the Hawaiian newspapers during 1865 through 1870, occasionally refers to Eepa. In the translations of his articles made for Bishop Museum by Martha W. Beckwith and Mary K. Pukui, a section relating to fishing narrates the legendary origin of the basket trap used for catching the small fish called *hinalea*. This trap was first made by an Eepa named Kalamainuu to trap two men who had betrayed to her husband the secret of her Eepa nature. The following summary of the story as told by Kamakau illustrates that supernatural beings who had the power of assuming many different transformations were labeled Eepa.

Kalamainu'u lived at Makaleha in the Waialua district on Oahu. She had a cave on the west side of Wailea Valley. She was really a *mo'o*, a "serpent," with a long, detachable tongue, which she later gave to her husband to use as a surfboard. He was Puna-'ai-koa'e, a descendant of chiefs of Kauai, who lived at Kapa'a in Puna. A skilled surfer, he was out one day surfing. He saw a beautiful woman on a long board and jumped on it to make love to her. By her power she drew him out to sea and then around to shore near her home. The two went to the woman's Wailea cave, where for several months they remained making love until the young man lost his good looks and yearned for the waves of his native land. He told his wife, "sitting with her bright hair streaming, reddened and shining," that he wanted to go surfing. She pointed to a board for him to take, but warned him against talking to two men whom he would meet on the way to the water.

He met two men and ignored their attempts to talk to him until they ran after him and declared that he would die if he did not listen to their advice. He stopped and said that perhaps his wife would not know that he had disobeyed her instructions. The men told him that she knew everything because she was a goddess, "a *mo'o*, one of the 40,000 *mo'o*, of the 400,000 *mo'o* group." The informers added, "That is the kind of body she has (a *mo'o* body). Your surfboard is her tongue." To be saved, he must go to Hawaii, where Pele was, but first he must return home, where his Eepa wife would show him her various divine bodies. He must take the exhibition calmly or she would kill him.

Kalamainu'u, angry with the two informers, pursued them until she got tired and went to sleep in the sun. Her servants found her and told her to make a certain type of basketry fish trap to catch the tattlers, Hinale and Akilolo. This she did, and when she had caught them she tore them to pieces and they became *hinalea* fish. Now Kalamainu'u is the *aumakua* (ancestral guardian spirit) for basket fishing in the place where the two deaths occurred.

Elsewhere, Kamakau discusses the Eepa bodies of the spirits and has more to say of Kalamainuu. He writes that her basic form was that of a *mo'o,* one of the supernatural creatures with "terrifying bodies," not to be identified merely with lizards or geckos. The *mo'o* gods, who brought material welfare and good catches of fish to their worshippers, were originally human beings, who became gods and assumed Eepa bodies. "These are constantly worshipped," writes Kamakau, "and the dead are offered to become such *eepa* bodies, but not just by burying them along the stream or river or beside a spring or by throwing the bones into the water (as some claim); if they have no right to the body of the *moʻo,* the bird, the shark, their bones will not take that form." The gods must come and carry off the corpses of those whom they accept as future *moʻo,* who then "have places where they lay aside those strange *eepa* bodies, but their nests are not known and the place where these *eepa* bodies abide." When a chief was to be dedicated to becoming a *moʻo,* the corpse or the bundle of bones wrapped in yellow tapa was taken to the offering place, "together with a dog of reddish brown, dark brown, or brindled color to be laid with the body in the water. By the time that the pig and the native dog were cooked in the imu and the all-important awa was ready to feed to the many-bodied *eepa* beings and the oven was ready to be opened, there lay the fearful bodies of those beings, great and small, in the water. The awa was given them to drink and they were fed with the dog and all the other food while the kahuna prayed and then carried the bundle and placed it in front of the *aumakua* to whom the body had been dedicated and it was borne away." Later the spirit would appear before the family, asking that they eat and drink and call on him in order to make him into a strong and powerful *aumakua.*

During sickness, people who had *moʻo* as spirit protectors, being related to Kalamainuu, offered the *moʻo* a reddish-brown or dark-brown dog, yellow tapa, and ʻawa root. These offerings were deposited in deep fresh-water ponds with prayers for health.

The two women from whom the tricky hero, Maui, stole the secret of fire had *"eʻepa"* forms, those of mudhens, which they assumed in trying to escape from Maui's clutches, according to a version given by Kamakau. He also describes the ancient goddess Papa as assuming many different bodies to woo her descendants after her husband Wakea is unfaithful to her. A descendant named Kio is said to have escaped the Eepa woman, presumably Papa, and married a woman of his own age group.

Kamakau tells the story of Laka and his search for his lost father in a most general way without giving the incident of the little people helping him to make his canoe. However, the historian does speak, during the course of his discussion of Laka, about the "home of the *eepa* people" as if this were a detail important to the story. In a note to her translation, Beckwith remarks that on Maui in 1930 Jonah Kaiwaaea of Kipahulu showed her where the tree for Laka's canoe was cut, the location of the stone table of the Eepa, the landing place from which the expedition started, and other places associated with the story of Laka. The implication is that the Eepa were involved in the story of Laka. Nothing is said of the Menehune, however, hence it seems to me that probably in the complete story, the Eepa were the little builders of Laka's magical canoe.

In Kamakau's account, it will be noted, the term *e'epa* is used primarily as an adjective describing the transformations of body achieved by supernatural beings who had once been human and had, after death, been accepted by the other supernatural beings as one of them. Eepa as the name for a group of spirits then would mean any with shape-shifting power, a power used by the fire-guarding mudhens and by Kalamainuu to disguise their supernatural nature from others or to escape from them. (Deformed human beings were always called Eepa.) The inclusion of Eepa in the Laka story suggests a later specialization of the term as the name of woodland guardians with supernatural qualities. The next step, to judge from the following myth, is to link them with Menehune.

According to an Oahu myth, the Eepa and the Menehune were delegated to build canoes for Chief Kahanai of Oahu who wished to visit Ku and Hina, his divine parents. He is, perhaps, the same as Kahanaiakeakua, for whom the Menehune built Kaheiki Heiau. The Menehune finished theirs on time, but the Eepa arrived late. It will be recalled that later both the Menehune and the Eepa were banished from Nuuanu Valley for their noisiness, which frightened the spirits bringing the two trees which were to serve as delicatessens.

The aforementioned heiau, called Kawaluna, at Waolani was a city of refuge for the sick and infirm; here, according to Kamakau (McAllister, 47, p. 85), came the sore-eyed, the crippled, the lame, the baldheaded, and the humpbacked. It looks as if the pathetic human beings who sought refuge at Kawaluna in Waolani have, with the passing of time, become romanticized into peculiar woodland spirits called the Eepa and then affiliated with the Menehune.

All of these bands of odd little people, the Mu, the Wa, the Wao, and the Eepa apparently belong to the innumerable *akua,* the innumerable spirits, whom the Hawaiians count by the 40's, the 400's, the 4,000's, and the 400,000's, as mentioned in the foregoing quotations from the native Hawaiian newspapers. These innumerable spirits occupied the woodland areas, and prayers invoked them en masse to make sure not one was skipped and insulted. These innumerable spirits are known and similarly counted in central Polynesia.

Thrum's translation (63, p. 113) of the Menehune chant given when they come to restore the tree Laka has chopped down follows:

> O the four thousand gods,
> The forty thousand gods,
> The four hundred thousand gods,
> The file of gods,
> The assembly of gods!
> O gods of these woods,
> Of the mountain,
> And the knoll,
> At the water-dam,
> Oh, come!

The Eepa and the Menehune belong to the forests and deep valleys where they control the woodland behavior of people from the flats. The Menehune controlled Laka's tree-cutting and canoe-building, and helped Eternal Fire pick mountain flowers. The Mu, Wa, and Wao (under the terms Kuamu, Kuawa, and Kuawao) were invoked in dedicating a new heiau; and when people went to the mountains to gather leaves for sacred purposes and to cut trees from which idols were to be carved, the returning procession chanted to these spirits as it marched home (Fornander, 27, vol. 6, pt. 1, pp. 52-55). It is said that when a tree is cut, the Mu are silent, the Wa are noisy (the name means noisy), while the Wao do as they please (Malo, 49, pp. 219, 238).

Other Hawaiian little people are the Haa-kualiki who are strong, valorous, and dwarfish (Malo, 49, p. 266), and the Kanaka-pilikua, dwarfs who are famous as runners. Chief Wahanui of Oahu brought some dwarfs to Kauai from a land of unidentified dwarfs said to have been known to ancient Hawaiians. One dwarf who was brought to Hawaii was called either an *ili* (small piece of land) or a *pilikua* (back-clinger) (Fornander, 26, vol. 2, p. 57; Beckwith, 5, p. 338).

Five Myths and Theories about the Origin of the Menehune

Five myths or traditions refer to the origin of the Hawaiian Menehune. Two tell of a great flood, and one of them, the Kumuhonua tradition, has been used by scholars like Fornander and Buck in reconstructing Polynesian history of the pre-European period. The other three myths, which are scarcely mentioned in such reconstructions, if at all, will be presented before the flood stories.

A major tradition about the origin of the little people is the Kanehunamoku legend (Thrum, 67, pp. 140-147). For trespassing in the flower garden of Kaonahi and making love to her, Kanehunamoku is banished, together with Kaonahi, by his parents, Kane and Kanaloa, to live on Kueihelani Island. Located in the clouds, the island floats about at night. It has three strata, and the stratum where the couple live is named for the island itself. Vast numbers of pygmy Menehune and Mu-ai-maia live on the third stratum under Kanehunamoku's rule.

When, once upon a time, the island floated near to Kauai, some of the small people landed at Peleiholani and traveled to Laau. Later, Chief Ola of Kauai asked Kanehunamoku and the Menehune overseer, Papaenaena, for workmen to build a dam and watercourse. The overseer accepted the assignment, but he and the other residents of the floating island rejected the Kauai request for the beautiful princess of Kueihelani. After the Menehune Ditch was finished, the Mu and the Menehune returned to the floating island, except for two Mu who overslept and were left behind. The story does not say what became of these two forlorn sleepyheads.

The Kanehunamoku myth, which has not been used in reconstructing Hawaiian and Menehune history, has apparently been accepted as a romantic tale. It is interesting to mark the fact that here both the Mu and Menehune are, by implication, credited with building the famous Menehune Ditch. The beautiful idea of a triple-decker island which floats about the clouds at night has been incorporated into the Kumuhonua myth to be discussed below. It is therein interpreted as being the Eden from which Kumuhonua, the first man, and his wife were driven for violating tapus, one of which was the eating of Kane's sacred mountain apple (Beckwith, 5, p. 67; Buck, 13, pp. 246-248).

The next two of the five traditions about the origin of the Menehune trace them to Kahiki, identified by some translators as Tahiti, although it often refers to a mythical Never-never Land. A third tradition also puts them temporarily on Kahiki, which, however, is identified by the narrator as New Zealand.

Kahano-a-Newa, a sorcerer, "stretched out his hands to the farthest bounds of Kahiki," and on them the Menehune came to Oahu, where they were given as dwelling places Kailua in the Koolau district and Pauoa and Puowaina in the Kona district. As servants of the woman Kahiki-ku-o-ka-lani, they built the six heiaus on Oahu which Fornander lists and which are given above. According to Fornander (26, vol. 2, p. 23) "the mention of the *Menehune* as servants of a chiefess of known southern extraction marks the legend as a product of that southern element, especially Tahitian, where *Menehune* had become the name for the lowest labouring class of the people." He interprets Kahiki as Tahiti. Cartwright, in an article in the Journal of the Polynesian Society (vol. 38), gives a version naming Kahana-a-ke-akua as the Oahu ruler whose servants were the Mu, Wa, and the Menehune. This is probably the same chief, Kahanaiakeakua, for whom the Menehune built Kaheiki Heiau and a canoe for his trip to visit his divine parents, Ku and Hina.

The above legend, told by Fornander, certainly is sufficiently unconnected with the other myths of Menehune origin as to mark it as a separate invention of Oahu and peculiar to it. Aside from the fanciful detail about workers from Kahiki being magically transported to Oahu by using a sorcerer's arm as a bridge between the islands, the story has a matter-of-fact quality which makes it sound like an account of an early effort to meet a labor shortage—a problem which was to face European developers of the islands in later times and which was also solved by importing workmen. However, Cartwright's version shows its folkloristic basis by the extension of the story to include the Mu and the Wa with the Menehune as the servants of another royal person.

The next tradition tracing the Menehune to Kahiki tells of Paao, a Samoan priest, coming to the Hawaiian Islands by way of Kahiki, translated as Tahiti, where he gathered followers called Manahuna or Manahuna-nuku-mu (Bugmouthed-Manahuna) because of their dainty mouths. The narrator, however, did not consider these people to be the same as the Menehune (Green, 31, p. 121). As the Mookini Heiau on Hawaii is said to have been built by Paao and as it is credited by some narrators (but not all) to Menehune workmen, it is curious that no narrator has united these two separate traditions and accepted the Manahuna as the same as the Menehune (Fornander, 26, vol. 2, pp. 36-38, 53; Thrum, 61, p. 117). Only the above account, one of the several versions of the Paao tradition, even mentions the Manahuna, and therefore suggests that they are its narrator's inventive addition to the story. Opinions differ as to whether Paao was originally from the Society Islands or from Samoa (Stokes, 56, pp. 40-45).

The spelling of the name of the followers as "Manahuna" indicates central Polynesian influence in the story, for the Tahitian dialectical form of the name Menehune is Manahune. The narrator, in rejecting the relationship of Manahuna and Menehune, indirectly attests to the Manahuna story having a different origin from those about the Menehune. The terms, although ultimately related, have been different for so long that, as far as the narrator is concerned, the legends have a quite different genealogy, so to speak. To him the stories are psychologically and genetically distinct and relate to different people.

FLOOD STORIES

Quoting, he states, from "Ke Kumulipo," the ancient Hawaiian tradition "handed down for countless generations," Akina (Rice, 52), narrates that until a great flood destroyed it, there was a vast Pacific continent which included all of what is now Polynesia and Fiji. The flood covered the lowlands of the continent and left exposed the highlands which became islands; then the ocean filled in the lowlands permanently. Many people were saved from death in this flood by a powerful magician named Nuu (Noah).

I have a couple of fanciful suggestions about this myth and offer them to the next narrator. What do we have here but a suggestion of the notorious lost continent of Mu? I have always wondered who the Mu for whom this continent is named was. Now, after studying the Menehune and their relatives the Mu, the Wa, the Wao—and don't forget, the Eepa—I think that, from a literary point of view, they obviously belong on the lost continent of Mu. After all, Lydgate's informant said that the Mu antedated the Menehune, and in Akina's version they are rulers of the Menehune, so this lost continent of Mu, with full poetic and political justice, must have been their ancient homeland. The Menehune Protective Association may do what they can to change it to the lost continent of the Menehune.

But let us return to Akina's charming story. Three groups of people survived the flood. They were the dwarfish Menehune, Kenamu (The Mu), and Kenawa (The Wa), but the Menehune later destroyed most of the other two groups. The three bands were energetic travelers, for they went from Kauai to Kahiki, here interpreted as New Zealand, and back. From New Zealand to Kauai came the Kenamu grandfather of Ola. Remember, it was for Ola that the Menehune built the Waimea watercourse.

Long before the birth of Ola on Kauai, Akina's account continues, the Menehune had gone to New Zealand with their king and chief, returning when they heard of Ola's birth. This was during the time of Hema, the great hero and progenitor of the Maori. Even before their departure from Kauai to New Zealand, rocks and other mementos of their occupation were visible. On their return they performed many more great deeds and spread through the valleys of Kauai as their numbers increased greatly. They were Ola's workmen, and in addition to building the watercourse, they built for him Hauola Heiau and roads, planted taro patches, and prepared a large earth oven. Later, however, when the people began to marry Hawaiians, the Menehune king ordered the exodus from Kauai to a place not disclosed. This, in essence, is the history of the Menehune after the Deluge, as told by J. A. Akina to the Reverend W. H. Rice.

Most of the native names which were omitted in the above account to keep the sequence of events clear are assembled below with the available translations.

The flood	Kai-a-ka-hina-alii	The-sea-that-made-the-chiefs-fall-down
The continent	Ka-houpo-o-Kane	The-solar-plexus-of-Kane
The ocean	Moana-nui-kai-oo	Great-engulfing-ocean
Ola's grandfather	Kaulu-nui-kini-akua	Big-Kaulu-of-the-four-thousand-gods
Ola's father	Kaulu-nui-pauku-moku-moku	Big-Kaulu-of-the-broken-rope
Kauai	Kauai-a-mano-ka-lani-po or Ka-ma-wae-lua-lani-nei	
New Zealand	Kahiki-moe or Kapaia-haa	
Menehune king	Ma-oli-ku-laiakea or Maori-tu-raiatea	
Maori place name	Raiatea	
Menehune chief and wife	Aliikilola and Lepoa	

The name of Ola's father is later mistakenly given as the name of the head-man sent by the young chief's father to call the Menehune back to Kauai from New Zealand.

The account of the Menehune which Akina professes to have taken from the Kumulipo apparently takes them up to the time of their return to Kauai from New Zealand, whereas he seems to have acquired the information about the later events from sources other than the Kumulipo.

Thrum does not accept Akina's version of the history of the Kauai Menehune. He writes (70, p. 84):

> The party furnishing Mr. Rice the Menehune stories of this collection had worked out a very plausible and scholarly theory, claiming that it emanated from the "Kumulipo" tradition of Creation, purporting to show that after the Deluge there were three people. . . . This account is the only authority we have for the story of their departure, attributed to the solicitude of their king for the purity of his race. Many of them having taken Hawaiian wives, he decided to leave the islands, so he summoned them all and took departure for New Zealand.
>
> Unfortunately for the would-be scholar, his version will not check up, for with the exception of Hema, all names given in his account are absent in the Kumulipo source material.

To make an incidental comment, the account in Rice does not state, contrary to Thrum's remarks, where the Menehune went. The reference to their going to New Zealand does not apply to their final exodus from Kauai, it seems to me, but to their first trip from which they returned to Kauai to serve the young Ola.

Judging from Thrum's statement above, Akina, rather than handing on an ancient tradition unaltered, took, as narrators do more often than readers of Polynesian mythology wish to believe, a narrator's privilege of working out a theory and reassembling material which until then had existed in separate incidents united only by relating to the Menehune. The account indicates that he assembled all the scattered incidents that he knew about these little people and placed them in a modern framework of the tradition about the Deluge. And to complete the organized plot and explain the present absence or rarity of Menehune on an island where they did so much, he invented the part about the exodus. He could have used more material from the Kumuhonua myth (p. 38), to which his Deluge account is related, and thus have had the Menehune depart because of the cruelty of a chief and their desire to live in the Promised Land across the Red Sea of Kane. Instead, he completely revamped the story of the exodus and attributed their departure to racial pride.

More than any other account of the Menehune, Akina's charming narrative has served to establish the Menehune pattern of behavior and appearance in the public mind. If, as the first to collect and publish myths about the Menehune as little people, Thrum is called "the father of the Menehune," Akina, who followed in Thrum's footsteps, deserves to be called the "big brother of the Menehune." He brought together scattered and disconnected anecdotes and beliefs about the Kauai Menehune and creatively reinterpreted them.

In reply to my remark that much of the information in Akina's narrative about the social organization and games of the Menehune struck me as reminiscent of David Malo's descriptions of Hawaiian customs in "Hawaiian antiquities," Kenneth Emory drew my attention to the fact that Akina, after all, belongs to a fairly recent period and might well have drawn on Malo, as many

Hawaiians did, to supplement his knowledge about the past history and vanishing customs of his race. But there the resemblance to Malo ends, for the absence of any reference by Malo to the Menehune points either to their unimportance or to the rarity or absence of myths about them at the time that Malo wrote about Hawaiian customs. Akina's interest in the Menehune was perhaps renewed by the publication of Thrum's work, leading him to assemble and revise the Kauai stories of the little people.

The Deluge framework used by the Kauai narrator bears evidence of having been influenced by the Biblical account and, therefore, of having been added to the old Menehune myths. A destructive deluge is not an unusual natural phenomenon, and stories about floods occur in Polynesian mythology. Independent of historical connection and due only to observation of natural phenomena, flood myths occur in many parts of the world. Independent origin is indicated by the few similarities in versions from widely separated geographical areas—few similarities, that is, beyond those which would almost inevitably arise from the nature of the subject. However, when the similarities extend to names of places and characters as well as to such other details in the plot as are clearly artificial embellishments of the story, evidence of contact among the narrators is indicated. These contacts may occur after the independent origin of each tradition, in which case narrators may try to harmonize the differing versions. Because the Biblical version of the Deluge is fixed in writing and has great prestige, the native narrator often tries to adapt it to the pre-existing mythology of his people, or he simply incorporates it by translating the names and re-naming the places. The process of harmonizing native and Biblical traditions, not only of the Flood but of Creation, is very evident in the next Menehune myth to be discussed.

Most quoted as evidence that the Menehune are the aborigines of the Hawaiian Islands are variants of the myth about the first man, Kumuhonua, who was made from earth, and his wife, who was made from one of his ribs. The myth continues through the events of the banishment of the couple from the land of Kane, the creator god, for having eaten Kane's sacred mountain apple at the instigation of a white bird. Later the sinfulness of the people leads to their destruction in a great flood. Nuu and his wife received a great canoe from Kane and were saved; and after the flood was over, Nuu sacrificed an animal to Kane. Later, people oppressed by Chief Wahanui were led by Kanaloa and Kaneapua, priests of Kane, to the land of Kane after passing over the Red Sea of Kane, which parted at the stroke of Kaneapua's staff.

Fornander states that in this myth he synthesized the traditions given by the Hawaiian historians, Kamakau and Kepelino (27, vol. 6, pt. 2, pp. 266-271, 277, 349; and 26, vol. 1, pp. 23, 24, 97-99, 132-134, 137, 160-161, 182-183, 209; vol. 2, pp. 13, 19). The Menehune in this synthesis are described as "the ancestors of the present Hawaiian people" and descendants of Kupulupulu;

the Nawao or Mu (the terms are used synonymously) are descendants of Kupulupulu's older brother. In another version, their father, Lua Nuu (who has many other names) is said to be the father of the progenitor of the Menehune, Kalani Menehune, by his wife Mee Hiwa, while the progenitor of the Wao, Ku Nawao, was the offspring of his slave wife, Ahu. Lua Nuu is in the twenty-third generation from Kumuhonua and in the tenth generation from Nuu who anchored his ark on Maunakea after the flood was over.

Kepelino appears to have contributed no information about the Menehune to Fornander's synthesis, for they are not even mentioned in the traditions recorded by the Hawaiian historian and published in 1932 by the Bishop Museum. Nor are the Mu or Wa mentioned. However, the Nawao appear as the people of Kanaloa, high priest of Kane. Thrum (70) states that Kamakau does not mention the Menehune, except to credit them with building certain heiaus. In the translations of Kamakau's articles stored in the Bishop Museum, I have found only one reference to the Menehune, in which he names Mauoki Heiau as having been erected by them. He writes: "Menehuna [were] a numerous race of men often spoken about in stories of old days. They were innumerable in number. Kahananuialewa is said to have brought them here. He was a man with stretching power in his arm. Mauoki was constructed by the Menehuna out of stones from Kawiwi in Waianae. Each one of the Menehuna is said to have brought one stone until Mauoki was completed. The race are called Menehuna by the ancients and they are said to have come from the east." This is a variant of a story given earlier (p. 34).

Kepelino and Fornander tell of an exodus of certain tribes into the Promised Land. According to Fornander, the Menehune were oppressed by Chief Wahanui (Chief Big-mouth) of Honuailalo (Southern Land), and escaped to a happier home. Kepelino states that the Nawao were oppressed. They lived either at Kona, Hawaii, or mythical Kahiki-honua-kele. Kane, god of the oppressed people, sent the brothers, Kanaloa and Kaneapua, to lead them to the "Bosom-of-Kane" across the Red Sea of Kane. The brothers led them "over the sea and through the wilderness" with Wahanui on their heels. At the Red Sea, Kaneapua struck the water with his staff and the people crossed over into the Promised Land. In their new land, people observed certain tapu days and made offerings of sheep and swine.

In the sixth generation from Kalani Menehune and the thirtieth from Kumuhonua, the Hawaiian Adam, appears Hawaii-loa or Hawaii-nui, putative discoverer of the Hawaiian Islands and "ancestor of the Hawaiians." According to Kepelino, this leader went from Kahiki-honua-kele and discovered all the Hawaiian Islands. He settled on Hawaii and named the other islands after his children who later settled them. (No Menehune are mentioned.) According to Fornander, only Hawaii and Maui had emerged from the ocean when

Hawaii-loa arrived, but before he died, the other lands arose from the water and were divided among the leader's children, whose names the islands bear.

A tradition given in 1904 by a Hawaiian (Beckwith, 4, p. 180), states that a man, Ka-menehune, and a woman, Opea-menehune, were born from the knees of Ku-ka-polipolipo, the first woman in the world. The two became human beings at a mythical place called Po-kinikini. All this took place in the land of Kane. Another story (Beckwith 4, 187) names Laka, a girl, and Menehune, a boy, as the children of Pele, the fire goddess, and her husband Wahieloa. In both accounts the name of Menehune appears to be used merely as a personal name. The stories have not been used to explain the origin of the Menehune as a people.

OTHER THEORIES OF MENEHUNE ORIGIN

Of the five traditions, only the Kumuhonua account seems to be used to support the theory, which has been most elaborated by Fornander and Buck, that the Menehune were the *kama'aina* of the Hawaiian Islands, the first human beings to occupy the islands.

Fornander (26, vol. 1, pp. 55-57, 98-100, 137, 161) writes that although the Polynesians were called the Menehune in the Kumuhonua tradition, the name was dropped as a national appellation so long ago "that subsequent legends have converted it into a term of reproach, representing the Menehune people sometimes as a separate race, sometimes as a race of dwarfs, skillful labourers, but artful and cunning." Menehune means literally, he states, "people of Mene." The name Mene, he finds, occurs also among the Arabs and Egyptians. This suggests to him that the Polynesians, Arabs, and Egyptians once shared a common national existence, traditions, and legends. The Semitic origin of the Polynesians is a major part of Fornander's theory, and he cites many customs and traditions which he regards as similar among the Polynesians and the western peoples.

At first, he writes, he believed the Kumuhonua tradition to be a "paraphrase or adaptation of the Biblical account by some semi-civilized or semi-Christianized Hawaiian, after the discovery of this group by Captain Cook." Later, through the study of Hawaiian folklore, he came to feel "that, though the details of the legend, as narrated by the Christian and civilized Kamakau, may possibly in some degree, and unconsciously to him, have received a Biblical coloring, yet the main facts of the legend, with the identical names of places and persons, are referred to more or less distinctly in other legends of undoubted antiquity. I am compelled, therefore, to class the legend among the other Chaldaeo-Arabico-Hebraic mementos which the Polynesians brought with them from their ancient homelands in the West . . ." However, he could not accept the historicity of the Hawaii-loa legend in its existing versions, for he felt it represented "the concentration of several originally distinct legends upon one person," some of these legends being about persons, "partly pure Cushites, partly Cushite-Polynesians."

Fornander, in short, regards the Kumuhonua tradition as having been brought by the Polynesians from an ancient, Asiatic, Semitic homeland. From this hypothetical homeland, he states, also comes what he calls the old name of the Polynesians—Menehune—a name, he adds, that has been debased by later storytellers. The Hawaii-loa legend which belongs with the Kumuhonua tradition has not been well-preserved, Fornander writes, for it now represents a fusion of different stories about different heroes, some, perhaps, of great antiquity. The Menehune, according to Fornander's theory, are not only the *kama'aina* of the Hawaiian Islands but of all Polynesia, since anciently Menehune was the name of the Polynesians. As supplementary evidence, Fornander refers to its application to Tahitian commoners.

In a popular book, Buck (13, pp. 59, 246-252) discusses how Kamakau and Kepelino incorporated post-European, Christian elements, especially from the Old Testament, into their versions of the Hawaiian traditions. Unlike Fornander, Buck is skeptical of the antiquity of much of the information in these Christianized traditions, but recognizes that Kepelino and Kamakau did retain some old, native elements which belong to the traditional stock-in-trade of many Polynesian islands. Like Fornander, he regards the Hawaii-loa tradition with much suspicion and suggests that the tradition-keepers gave him the name of the island to establish their claim that he was the first settler.

Doubtless for the sake of literary continuity and popular interest, Buck often blends old myths and new theories into a historical reconstruction of the main events in the career of the pre-European Polynesians. He thus reconstructs the history of the Menehune and their culture. It is easy in following the interesting hypothesis to ignore the restrictive adverbs that the author, with scientific caution, injects at frequent intervals and to overlook which information he credits to myth and which to theory. In a later popular article on the origin of the Hawaiians and their culture (14, pp. 6-8), he presents parts of the same reconstruction but with fewer restrictive adverbs. In an even later, scientific monograph (15, pp. 475, 477), he simply uses the term Menehune as the name of the earliest Hawaiian settlers, whose culture, he states, was replaced by that of newcomers who absorbed them.

According to Buck's reconstruction of early Polynesian history, the Menehune were real people of Polynesian stock who set out from Tahiti and discovered and settled the Hawaiian Islands. He states that the people who came with Hawaii-loa were Menehune, but the source of this specific tradition I have not located. Apparently it is Buck's deduction derived from his synthesizing of the Kumuhonua legend quoted by Fornander wherein both Hawaii-loa and the Menehune are described as ancestors of the Hawaiians. As he is in the sixth generation from the original progenitor of the Menehune, the mythical Hawaii-loa himself must have been a Menehune and presumably his traveling companions were of his own band. Thus one arrives at the interpretation that the Menehune first came to Hawaii with its discoverer, a Menehune leader whose name has been forgotten and who has been given the name of the island he discovered and settled. Thus, he and the Menehune were the first Hawaiians. Perhaps the same line of reasoning led Fornander to identify the Menehune as "the ancestors of the present Hawaiians." Buck, however, identifies the ancestors of the present Hawaiians as people who came later than the Menehune from the Society Islands.

In a recently published book (The coming of the Maori, 1950), Buck goes a step farther, for he identifies the Menehune as the long-headed people, whom physical anthropologists regard as predecessors of a broad-headed population in Polynesia.

Most of Buck's hypotheses of Tahiti as the homeland of the Menehune are linked with the possibility of their having lived at one time on Necker and Nihoa, barren and rocky islets at the northwestern end of the Hawaiian Islands. Before continuing this summary of Buck's reconstruction of Menehune history, it is essential to review Emory's research on Necker and Nihoa, for Buck's theory of Menehune residence there is derived from it (24, especially pp. 116-122).

At the time of historic discovery, Necker and Nihoa were unoccupied by human beings, though both had archeological remains, showing them to have had human inhabitants at one time. Necker was unknown to Hawaiians during the early historic period, but they knew of Nihoa from a tradition said to have inspired the wife of Kaumualii of Kauai (the same king whose census taker counted 65 Menehune in Laau) to send an expedition to seek the mysterious islet. However, at some past period Hawaiian fishermen and birdcatchers used to visit Nihoa, for Emory found evidences of their brief sojourns. Indications from what they lost or abandoned are that they had a different culture from that of the people who built the heiaus now in ruins on the islet.

On the basis of his survey, Emory believes that the Necker culture was "a pure sample of culture prevailing in Hawaii before the thirteenth century." He also sees traces of it on Nihoa and, to a slight extent, on Kauai. This culture had come, he states, from the Society Islands. A major point of evidence was the similarity between the Necker type of heiau and that of inland Tahiti. This type is believed to belong to an early phase of Tahitian culture and to its settlers whom he calls Manahune, the name of the Tahitian commoners. Thus, before the thirteenth century, Tahiti and the Hawaiian Islands had, according to Emory, a culture with many similarities to that which survived for a while on Necker and which in Tahiti was that of the Manahune.

The Manahune settlers of Tahiti, Emory's theory continues, were conquered by their Raiatean neighbors; were reduced to commoner status; and had a new culture imposed upon them. One of the new culture elements was a different type of temple. Society Islands immigrants who had this new culture invaded the Hawaiian Islands during the twelfth or thirteenth century and succeeded in introducing it. Incidentally, Mookini Heiau on Hawaii, which is attributed to Paao and the Menehune, is an example of the new type of temple. Emory believes that "people of the Necker cult were forced out of the main Hawaiian group and settled for a time on Nihoa." As very few skeletal remains were found on Necker and Nihoa, one may well ask, as did the investigator, what became of the small permanent or semi-permanent population of about 100 people who are assumed to have resided at some time on these barren, almost waterless islands.

Emory's reconstruction of the history of Necker and Nihoa culture, it should be pointed out, particularly as to the invasion of the Hawaiian Islands by Society Islanders in the twelfth or thirteenth century, draws on Fornander's reconstruction of Polynesian prehistory.

To return to Buck's reconstruction, he favors a Tahitian origin for the Menehune because of the connections between the Necker culture and the early Tahitian culture of the first settlers, called Manahune by Emory. The basic assumption in Buck's reconstruction is that the Menehune were the first people in the Hawaiian Islands. This point, it will be recalled, is implied only in the Kumuhonua tradition. They settled the islands and spread over them until later invaders from Tahiti, ancestors of the present Hawaiians, gradually pushed them out of the other islands of the group to the northernmost of the principal islands, Kauai. There, Buck continues, they congregated for a time, withdrawing finally even farther north to Nihoa and Necker, where they resided until they took to the sea again and vanished, as mysteriously as they did from Kauai in Akina's account, leaving behind much stonework but almost no bones.

Subsequent residents of the Hawaiian Islands, according to Buck, began to describe them as dwarfs because of the Polynesian tendency to praise their own ancestors and to belittle literally those who preceded them. Also, the newcomers, who had a higher standard of living and a better diet, were perhaps better built than the Menehune, who came to be regarded not merely as runts but as an actual race of dwarfs. Magical elements gathered around their reputation until historic fact was obscured.

Akina would probably have been interested in the Necker-Nihoa theory as an explanation of where the Menehune, led by their race-purist king, went on their great exodus from Kauai, though the more than 500,600 people would have raised the question of space. Maybe some moved to the multiple-decked floating island.

CRITICISM OF MENEHUNE-ORIGIN THEORIES

Other than Fornander and Buck, only Thrum has written at any length on the subject of the origin and nature of the Menehune. He quotes (62, p. 113), without comment, from Fornander on the Kumuhonua legend that the Polynesians are descendants of Lua Nuu's son named Menehune. However, Thrum (70) stresses the conflicting and confused opinions of the Hawaiians themselves about the origin, nature, and fate of the Menehune and the absence of references to them in the Hawaiian folklore recorded by Malo and their rarity in the papers of Kamakau. He points out how some Hawaiians, such as J. H. Kaiwi (42), regard the Menehune as contemporaneous with the sandalwood-collecting days of the European period, whereas to other Hawaiians, such as Moke Manu (Thrum, 62, p. 113), they were invisible, supernatural beings of unknown origin who were governed by someone higher in rank than themselves who assigned them to the mountains and hills and who, up to the time of Papa and Wakea (seven generations after Hawaii-loa and thirty-seven from Kumuhonua), were the only inhabitants of the islands. The only point of agreement which Thrum finds among Hawaiians is that there were Menehune in the islands (70, p. 87). The many discrepancies and erroneous claims refute the Hawaiian notion, he states, that the Menehune were an actual race of pygmies.

Typical inconsistencies in regard to time are the conflicts between Fornander's Kumuhonua legend and Akina's version. Akina has the Menehune living on Kauai immediately after the Deluge, which they survived. The Kumuhonua legend states that the ancestor of the Menehune was not born until at least a half dozen generations or more after the time of Nuu, who lived at the time of the Flood and saved some of the people.

As we have seen, the Menehune have been claimed as aborigines of the Hawaiian Islands almost exclusively on the basis of a synthesis by Fornander of versions of the Kumuhonua myth, which itself is a fusion of Christian European and native Hawaiian elements. Other evidence used to support this theory, is derived from the similarity between the Tahitian name for their lower classes, Manahune, and the Hawaiian name, Menehune.

Menehune has appeared as a personal name in the genealogies associated with the origin myths showing Christian influence. The identification of the Menehune as the ancestors of the Hawaiians is based on sketchy and uncertain evidence. Only the Kumuhonua myth identifies them in this way, and it is not absolutely certain that even it does, for the remark that the Menehune are the ancestors of the Hawaiians may represent Fornander's interpolation based on his view that the term Menehune was an old name for the Polynesians even before their immigration into the eastern Pacific. Of the native historians, neither Kepelino nor Malo mentions the name Menehune in any connection. Presumably Fornander's phrase, if not an interpolation, is from Kamakau, who, according to Thrum, familiar with Kamakau's as yet unpublished records, does not mention the Menehune except to credit them with having built certain heiaus.

Acceptance of the Kumuhonua myth as evidence that the Menehune were the early settlers of Hawaii rests on the belief that native traditions provide trustworthy accounts of real events, after first removing the Christian European incidents and names; smoothing out discrepancies; eliminating supernatural elements; and interpreting the metaphors, similes, and other Polynesian devices of figurative speech, in what the interpreter regards as matter-of-fact terms. Accompanying the acceptance of this myth by Fornander was his confidence in the ability of people to retain some historical truth in oral traditions supposedly handed down for generations and carried from the ancient homeland. Were one to remove obviously Christian European elements from the Kumuhonua legend, there would be little left but padded genealogies.

Confidence in the value of native traditions as sources of direct history has diminished in the last few years. Yet most of the major reconstructions in Polynesian research today still unwittingly incorporate elements from them. For the most part, this is done through failure to remember that much in the older hypotheses was based on inferences from the content of the myths. In other words, these hypotheses are used in the new theories.

Both Fornander and Buck reject as invention the Hawaii-loa myth. This mythical discoverer's forbears included the Menehune who are accepted in the theories as the ancestors of the Hawaiians because their mythical descendant and leader discovered the Hawaiian Islands. Yet the reality of the Menehune is as open to question as the reality of Hawaii-loa himself. About the only thing certain from the Hawaii-loa myth is that the Hawaiian Islands exist and were discovered and settled by Polynesians. But we have better proof of this than the myth.

Bits from the Kumuhonua myth also appear in the account of the Kauai Menehune given to Rice by Akina, but Thrum has pointed out the historical untrustworthiness of Akina's theory of Menehune origin and exodus. There is no reason why Polynesians should not fabricate any kind of myth that suits their esthetic and historical sense, or why Europeans should not enjoy them for whatever charm they have. However, the content of these myths does not constitute history. Statements in the Menehune myths that the Menehune, or the Mu, or the Wa, or the Wao were Hawaiian aborigines are as folkloristic in their origin as the statements that these people now are invisible, work only at night, and are two feet high.

There is no evidence of scientific value in the myths about the Menehune to argue for the theory that they are the *kamaʻaina* of the Hawaiian Islands. Nor need one consider as other than a bit of fiction the statement that the Mu are even more *kamaʻaina* than the Menehune.

Some Processes of Menehune Myth Development

The Hawaiian Menehune have been a legendary group for about 160 years, a generous minimum estimate which uses the period since Cook's discovery of Hawaii as the basis, although actual written references to them did not appear until about 50 to 60 years ago. Had the Menehune been a real, observable people, we should have expected early Europeans who visited Hawaii to have written about them, as they did about the Manahune and the Manaune of the south whom they actually saw in the flesh and called by name. The laboring plebeians called Manahune by Society Islanders are known to Hawaiians as Noa (common) or Makaainana, People-belonging-to-the-land, a term also used in the Marquesas.

The Makaainana, as described by Malo (47, p. 88), tilled the soil, did the fishing, and performed the labor of house-building, canoe-making, and heiau construction. But the Menehune got, and are still getting, the credit for what the Makaainana did. The labor of the latter people, a social class of real human beings, has been credited to the mythical Menehune. Slaves (Kauwa) belonged to a distinct, segregated class, which was marked by cringing demeanor and by tattooing between the eyes and the upper corners of the eyes. When no law breakers were available as sacrifices for the Hawaiian heiaus, a Kauwa, like a Tahitian Titi, was taken "as we would now go to the barnyard to pluck a chicken," according to Mary K. Pukui.

The Makaainana, then, are the common people who carried the burden of the labor on land and sea, in peace and war. Hawaiian storytellers have glamourously romanticized the working class in the myths about the Menehune. This is a remarkable literary development for Polynesia, because most of Polynesian mythology, at least of what has been collected and published, makes the chiefs and the chiefesses the heroes and heroines of the plots, for they were the patrons and supporters of the storytellers. In the Menehune myths, the workers are the heroes, and the chiefs who requisition their services to build watercourses, fishponds, and heiaus are secondary in the plots.

There is no way of knowing when, or under what circumstances, the name Menehune was introduced into the Hawaiian Islands; or for how long the Hawaiians have called the common people Makaainana; or, if in the past before the term Makaainana was adopted, the Hawaiian plebeian class was called Menehune, as in the south. To suggest a possibility, the word Menehune may even have been introduced into Hawaii from the south during the early historic period and given a false patina of antiquity by being inserted into the earliest period of a genealogy.

Thrum (70, p. 88) remarks, "It is likely that the various works attributed to the Menehunes were the labors of Hawaiians themselves in years long past and forgotten, and credited to the mythical race of pygmies so long that they had come to believe in them as a bona fide race with supernatural powers."

A major process in developing and maintaining the lively existence of the Menehune traditions is suggested in Thrum's statement. The Hawaiians have used it to explain the origin of stone structures, many now in ruins, the history of which they have forgotten or have never known.

Emory has twice observed the formation of accretions to the Menehune mythology through this process. In 1920, 30 years ago, he learned on Maui that Hawaiians were attributing to Menehune construction certain heiaus about which Thrum, ten years earlier, had been able to get traditional accounts that did not mention the Menehune as builders. These traditions apparently have been forgotten since Thrum's visit, or have not been passed on orally to younger Hawaiians, who are unfamiliar with Thrum's and Fornander's publications where the older traditions are recorded. Belief in the Menehune offers people of today an ever-ready explanation for the construction of the heiaus in their district, the origin of which they do not know.

While making an archeological survey of Lanai Island, Emory had a similar experience. He writes (23, p. 119), "The Hawaiian very often finds it convenient to attribute unexplainable or forgotten works to the activities of the menehunes. . . . On Lanai I had the opportunity of observing the spread of the tendency. A group of natives . . . were much interested in my description of petroglyphs but were unable to account for them. In this group was Alika George Nicholas . . . who remembered having seen the petroglyphs on Oahu at . . . (Koko Crater). . . . He said, in perfect sincerity, 'Those pictures were cut by the menehunes and likewise the pictures on Lanai.' The natives present accepted his explanation."

One of the reasons, perhaps, why the Menehune are closely identified with Kauai is that of all the islands in the group, the history of its stone structures is the least known and the most unsatisfactory, for "the legends are disconnected and the genealogies are few." (See Bennett, 6, p. 7.) The Menehune, then, provide a popularly acceptable explanation for these mysterious ruins. Once the association of the Menehune with a few ruins has been accepted, the legendary people constitute a magnet to attract explanations of the stone structures and of every odd stone or feature of the landscape.

As stated earlier, Thrum also thought that the works now attributed to the Menehune were those of older Hawaiians, whose connection with the building of the heiaus had been forgotten. These works, he said, had become so firmly connected with Menehune activity that people had begun to believe in the Menehune as real people of pygmy size who specialized in stonework.

A factor, significant in the historic period, in elaborating the Menehune tradition is the interest in it shown by newcomers of all races and nationalities.

For newcomers, it is easier and more fun to remember that the Menehune built all the heiaus and fishponds than to learn what may still be known of the actual individual history of each heiau and pond. The difficulty of remembering the many-syllabled names of little-known chiefs and chiefesses probably contributes to the ease with which the entertaining stories about the Menehune, reminiscent of European pixies and trolls, are adopted as satisfactory explanations. Very helpful too are the facts that individual Menehune are rarely named in the stories and that the Menehune usually function as a cohesive band. One need remember only a single, easy name to feel like a *kamaʻaina* as regards Hawaiian history and folklore. We may anticipate that an increasing number of odd rocks and heiaus will be attributed to the Menehune.

Another important process in developing the Menehune tradition has been the revamping of the Menehune to fit the stereotype of forest spirits, who are definitely supernatural. The Menehune have come to be identified by storytellers as relatives of the innumerable *akua,* the forest spirits, and have been given some of their qualities and peculiarities, such as invisibility, small size, the duty of protecting the forests, touchiness about the observation of forest tapus, and ability to finish jobs in one night. These qualities are associated with forest spirits all over Oceania. The converse has also occurred, with the stereotype of forest spirits being enriched by assigning Menehune traits and craft skills to the woodland guardians.

In Hawaiian forests, as Malo reports, are named bands of spirits like the Mu, the Wa, and the Wao. Westervelt subsumes the Mu and the Wa under the collective name of Eepa, who, however, may be regarded by other forestry experts as an independent, but related, group. Then there are thousands of nameless spirits whom Hawaiians invoke by the 4,000, the 40,000, and the 400,000, to insure not missing or insulting one.

The Hawaiian Menehune primarily are workers in stone. I believe that the canoe-building attributed to them in Hawaii is a late addition to their skills, resulting from storytellers' identification of them with the forest spirits who lived in secluded places and were the guardians of trees and the objects made from them. It is likely that storytellers began, independently of each other, to ascribe canoe-making and forest-guardian tasks to the Menehune because of a gradual, growing tendency in storytelling circles to absorb the Menehune into the forest-spirit stereotype. Besides Laka's canoe, the Menehune built canoes for two Oahu chiefs who, like Laka, needed them in their search for lost relatives, a favorite occupation of Polynesian heroes. Menehune also made canoes on Kauai, and even gave certain stones there the shape of canoes. One can only guess whether the Menehune first became canoe-makers to build Laka's canoe or the canoes of the Oahu chiefs.

In one myth, it will be recalled, the Menehune compete with the Eepa to provide a chief with canoes, and the Menehune get theirs done first. A familiar solution for storytellers who are faced with harmonizing two different versions based on the same theme and with choosing between two characters to perform the same deed is to take both and have them compete with each other in doing the task. This process often occurs in the myths about Maui. In some islands, only Ru is known as the raiser of the sky; in others, only Maui is known as the hero who lifted up the low sky; and in still others, both heroes are regarded as sky-raisers, in which event, the storyteller has several choices. He can select either Maui or Ru as the hero; he can have Ru try to raise the sky and fail to finish the job, which Maui then takes over and completes; or he can have the two work simultaneously. It seems to me that the same process has operated in regard to the Eepa and the Menehune in the Oahu myth about Chief Kahanai and his canoe which I mentioned earlier. The narrator has both bands build canoes, but he has the Menehune get theirs done first. In this myth, the Menehune are used by the storyteller to do work that customarily belongs to Eepa and their forest kindred. However, the narrator balances the score in the same myth by giving the Eepa the job of building a heiau, which is more commonly a Menehune job.

The tendency toward fusing, confusing, relating, and setting into competition these companies of odd, forest beings is also evident in regard to the Menehune and the Nawao. Narrators of the Bible-inspired Kumuhonua myth differ, it will be remembered, as to whether it was the Menehune or the Nawao who were persecuted by Chief Big-mouth and escaped to the promised land of Kane. One narrator, however, considers the two bands as descendants of brothers, a relationship which seems to me to represent an attempt to reconcile conflicting versions by a familiar literary device. If heroes are not identified as one and the same, they are interpreted as being relatives. On Kauai, there is a tendency to confuse the Mu-ai-maia and the Menehune. As Kaiwi points out, some of the things her grandparents credited to the Menehune are attributed by others to the Mu. Lydgate's account offers a characteristic solution in which the narrator declares that the two people are related to each other though the Mu are an earlier band than the Menehune.

Living in the same forest area in Laau, Kauai, are the Menehune, the Mu, and the Wao. The common residence assigned them represents one more step by the narrators in fusing the characteristics of these bands.

SUMMARY

After a review of the data on the investigation of the Menehune and of the development of the mythology about them, I suggest that the name Menehune is a central Polynesian word which was introduced into the Hawaiian Islands, where it received its present dialectical form. It may have been that of the common people of the Hawaiian Islands, as it was in the Society Islands, until it was replaced by the term Makaainana, which continued to be used into the days of the monarchy in European times. Makaainana is also used in the Marquesas, where no reference to Menehune has been reported. Another possibility is that the southern term, Manahune, was introduced into the Hawaiian Islands during the historical period but failed to displace Makaainana as the categorical term for commoners, and was, instead, adopted into the folklore as the name of a group of mythical workmen. Perhaps some other hypothesis would fit the case better. That the name Menehune may have been introduced more than once is suggested by the stories of Kahano-a-Newa and of Paao which are not thought to refer to the same people. At any rate, the name of Menehune and its association with laborers represent an introduction from the south into the Hawaiian Islands, a point here anticipated from research described in the next section.

The use of the name Menehune as a personal appellation is, as will be shown later, not unusual, for men named Menehune are known from central Polynesia. There is no need to interpret Kalani Menehune or any other Menehune-named individual on Hawaiian genealogies as ancestors of the band of people called Menehune, for the term can exist as a personal name without being eponymous.

Whatever happened immediately after the term Menehune diffused into the Hawaiian vocabulary is unknown, but it certainly did not survive or take hold as the categorical term for the working class of real people. How it first became connected with ancient stone structures is unknown, but the fact remains that it did. That this process was initiated on Kauai may be inferred from the great number of Menehune-associated places on that island, far greater than on any other island in the Hawaiian Archipelago. That Kauai should have more such places may be inferred from the fact that of all the islands the circumstances of the building of many of its stone structures are the least well-preserved; the process of crediting them to the Menehune, a shadowy people with a reputation for being workers, was established and has gained increasing momentum through the years, as the experiences of Thrum and Emory have demonstrated. It should also be added here that of all the islands Kauai is recognized by its neighbors as being the richest in stories and story-places.

Inevitably, storytellers must have asked themselves, or must have been asked, who the Menehune who did so much building were, what they looked like, where and how they lived, and whether anyone had ever seen them. The stereotype of the forest spirits provided some of the answers, for the attributes of elusiveness, nocturnal working hours, smallness of size, and forest habitat are typical of many other Oceanic spirits besides the Hawaiian Menehune, the Mu, the Wa, and the Wao. Once the Menehune have been identified with one or more bands of forest spirits, the next problem is to distinguish between these similar bands and determine what were their kinship and contacts. Then one must follow the various steps peculiar to inventive storytellers. The epithet of one band becomes the name of a new band; or the name of a band is defined as merely the epithet of another so that both are regarded as identical. The bands are regarded as related to each other through common ancestry. They are incorporated into the same stories by being set into competition with each other to perform a task, or they work cooperatively at various tasks.

The incorporation of the Menehune into the Bible-inspired myth about their being harassed by a cruel chief and eventually immigrating to a wonderful land is definitely a late addition, as is the entire Kumuhonua myth in which Hawaiian names and details are worked into a Biblical framework. The myth can surely be dismissed as regards information of historical value, but it remains as one of the most interesting examples of the mythological process of adopting and adapting new traditions into a mythology. The fact that one variant states that the harassed people were the Nawao whereas another states that they were the Menehune simply exemplifies the process of identifying these bands as being similar to each other. The whole myth is as fanciful as the floating island home of pygmy bands. In both myths, the Menehune and other bands of little people from the folklore have been incorporated to elaborate a story and fit it into a local setting. The formation of the framework of Akina's account of the Menehune on Kauai under the inspiration of the Kumuhonua myth and the episode of the flood, but with a different version of their exodus, also is more significant from the standpoint of the studies of creative change in mythology than of direct, source material on the history of Kauai.

THE MANAHUNE OF THE SOCIETY AND COOK ARCHIPELAGOES

Only for central Polynesia can we accept as sober fact the statements of any Europeans (or Polynesians, for that matter) that they have truly seen Menehune in the flesh. Captain James Cook, his naturalist, J. R. Forster, and other members of the crew are among the Europeans who became well-acquainted with the Manahune, not only of Tahiti, but of other islands in the Society Archipelago. Missionaries who followed the discoverers also knew real, live Manahune. Marvelous stories such as those told of the Hawaiian Menehune are not associated with the southern Manahune, though central Polynesian myths about supernatural beings share certain elements with those told of the Hawaiian Menehune. But perhaps something about the Hawaiian Menehune can be learned from studying the central Polynesian characters with the related name, and from the myths about supernatural beings like them.

Six Uses of the Term Manahune

The term Manahune (Manaune in the Cook Islands) appears in six major contexts in the Society, Cook, and Tuamotuan Archipelagoes. These contexts, which are discussed in the following pages, are summarized as follows:

1. The lowest class of the Society Islands into historic times.
2. The early settlers of Tahiti.
3. Any Society Islander, according to Tuamotuans of the historic period.
4. One of the eight or nine bands said to have accompanied the great chief, Tangiia, who settled in Rarotonga in the Cook Islands. It is believed that this band, which perhaps had the alternate name of Mangiia, later left Rarotonga, to settle on the island later called Mangaia, another of the Cook Islands.
5. A leading family in Mangaia which won the temporal rule of that island.
6. An epithet for (1) the islands of Tahiti and Moorea and (2) an ancestor of the Tahitian royalty.

THE MANAHUNE AS COMMONERS

The Manahune constituted the lowest of the three social classes in Tahiti, Raiatea, Moorea, and other islands of the Society Archipelago. Descriptions of these three major classes, as Williamson, who has assembled source material on them, points out (76, pp. 384-393), are confusing and conflicting. Although class boundaries were distinct in the Society Islands, they were not so strongly defined, Ellis states, as in the Hawaiian Islands (21, vol. 3, pp. 94-99). Each class had graded subdivisions, but it is often difficult to determine to which class a specific, named group of people belonged. Society Islanders perhaps differed on these details from island to island.

The three ranks of society, according to Ellis, were, first, the Hui Arii, the royal family to which belonged the king or the reigning chief of each island, the members of his family, and all who were related to them. Henry (36, pp. 229-230, 313) names two subdivisions of the royalty as the Arii Maroura, chiefs of the red girdle, and the Arii Rii, the petty chiefs.

The second rank of society was the Bue Raatira, according to Ellis; or the Hui Raatira, according to Henry. This class constituted the gentry, or the middle class of land owners, and those who occupied land in return for military services to the owner and for a part of the produce. The Raatira also consisted of various subdivisions, not very well defined, at least not in the source material. Middle class families varied greatly in wealth and authority.

The third rank of society was the Manahune, the plebeians. The subdivisions were not distinct. Tahitian artisans and fishermen were sometimes ranked with the Manahune but more often with the Raatira. They were a connecting link between the plebeian and the middle classes.

Ellis gives three subdivisions of the Manahune class, the distinctions being based primarily on function: (1) the Teuteu, servants of the upper classes; (2) the Titi, slaves who were prisoners of war or refugees; and (3) a group of landless, craftless, and dependent vassals, "all who were destitute of any land,

and ignorant of the rude arts of carpentering, building, etc., which were respected among them, and such as were reduced to a state of dependence upon
those in higher stations." (See 21, vol. 3, pp. 95, 96.) Fishermen and artisans,
it will be recalled, were classed sometimes with the Manahune but more often
with the Raatira. In Maupiti and Raiatea, Manahune and Raatira seem almost
synonymous, as will be discussed in a later section.

Like Ellis, Handy (34, pp. 7-8, 90, 103) describes the Tahitian Manahune
as landless commoners who lived as either tenants or serfs on the property of
the upper classes or occupied the inner valleys. They and their descendants
were called *noho vao,* "the dwellers in the far-away mountains and the *vao,* or
depths of the valleys." *Vao* is the dialectical equivalent of the Hawaiian word
wao. They were permitted to have a road to the seashore so that they could fish,
but they could not linger on the way. For their superiors, they picked taro
leaves, fished for eels and fresh-water fish, cut wood, planted gardens, paddled
canoes, and fought as soldiers in the wars.

From the standpoint of any possible connection, other than name, between
the Hawaiian Menehune and the southern Manahune, the important question
is whether the Manahune were artisans, like the Menehune, or unskilled
laborers. Ellis obviously rates the Manahune as unskilled (21, vol. 3, pp. 95,
96). So does Handy, except in a reference to the Manahune as the craftsmen
of the Arii in later times (34, pp. 10, 43). Captain Wilson of the missionary
ship, the *Duff,* observes (78, p. 333) that the Manahune served the Raatira
and the younger relatives of the chief by making cloth (tapa), building houses,
cultivating the land, helping with laborious tasks, and answering "all their
demands to the best of their ability."

The description of the Manahune given by J. R. Forster, Captain Cook's
naturalist, is more applicable to the usual account given of the Raatira (28, pp.
354-356, 371). Handy comments that apparently Forster did not understand
the difference between the two classes (34, p. 44). The social classes, according
to Forster, had a great chief at the head; members of his family were landed
proprietors and chiefs of districts; while the Manahune had "landed property,"
or grants of land which they cultivated themselves without Teuteu assistance.
They were also masters of war canoes or served on board them as warriors
while the Teuteu paddled. The duties of the Teuteu, as given by Forster, more
nearly fit the usual description of the functions of the majority of the Tahitian
Manahune, who cultivated the lands of others, fished, fed the dogs and hogs,
built houses and canoes, made tapa, worked on the boats in peace and war, and
did everything asked of them. In a sense, all the Manahune were Teuteu or
servants of the upper classes, but the term Teuteu seems more ordinarily to be
applied to domestics in the upper class households.

Williamson (76, p. 391), in attempting to reconcile the conflicting statements regarding the functions of the Manahune, suggests that they may have

done only the unskilled labor on the houses and canoes which Wilson and Forster said they built. It seems fairly clear that the southern Manahune, unlike the Hawaiian Menehune, were usually neither craftsmen nor artisans but unskilled laborers. "The crude labor in all work was . . . performed by *manahune*," according to Handy (34, p. 43).

The Titi appear to have been at the very foot of the social ladder. Although any Manahune or any obnoxious middle class man might be sacrificed in the temples of the chiefs, the Titi, like the Hawaiian Kauwa, were the usual source of human sacrifice, "fodder for the gods of war." They always ran the chance of being killed in revenge for battle losses suffered by their conquerors. Although never sold, they might be given away. Sometimes they were freed, in which case they might go home or elect to stay with their former owner. Those who had escaped death or capture on the battlefield or who feared they might be taken for the sacrificial altar sometimes got away to the mountain forests where they lived for years. Called Taehae, wild men, they were much feared by lowlanders who had work to do in the mountains. Ellis saw a Taehae who had been captured in 1821 and tells of others, including a band of men, women, and children (21, vol. 1, pp. 305-308 and vol. 3, p. 95; Henry, 36, pp. 196, 313; Handy, 34, p. 44). Gill also gives accounts, to be discussed later, of Taehae in Mangaia who were linked there with a family named Manahune.

In general, the attitude of the upper classes toward the Manahune, whatever their function, was one of contempt. Among the Manahune, those who were neither Titi nor Teuteu probably shared the prevailing hostile and contemptuous attitudes toward the slaves and the royal, hereditary servants.

The Teuteu, it is said, enjoyed "home-like privileges with their superiors" without infringing on their superiors' dignity, and took more liberties than other people (Henry, 36, p. 229). Some of these "ancient domestics [were] as much respected as their [the chiefs'] own relations, giving directions to the younger branches, and managing, as stewards, the affairs of the household without control."

Many Teuteu, however, were not so honorable. The subdivisions of the Manahune might be extended by listing those unpleasantly described thieves who were domestic favorites and constituted the harems of the king and queen (Wilson, 78, pp. 329, 333-334). Ellis (21, vol. 3, p. 130) writes vividly of how the Teuteu often used, without permission, the king's name to strip a household of everything it had; one man hid his canoe in the sand to avoid giving it to a Teuteu. Lieutenant de Bovis (10, p. 22) confirms the fact of the privileged position of royal servants and states that a Manahune who became a domestic in the Arii's household acquired a very great importance which reflected the power of the Arii he served. The Teuteu Manahune enjoyed a profitable racket, but in return they were despised and feared by all who were inferior to their royal masters.

The Titi also were despised, being called names meaning "human sacrifice" and "mean, low, or evil folk" (Handy, 34, p. 44).

The following is an insult to the Manahune as a whole (Handy, 34, p. 8) :

> Go to the mountains where you belong,
> Far, far away up there;
> Far away where the red skies lie,
> Away to the road of separation,
> Far away to the clustering yellow bamboos,
> Torch-fisher of the *nato* of Motutu,
> Picker of eels,
> Thou art the grandchild of the mountain,
> Thou slave of the Arii !

Manahune life had its brighter side. According to Henry (36, p. 229), they "made no pretensions to aristocracy. They served as retainers and workers for the upper classes, but also enjoyed their own hereditary possessions." But bondage was very gentle. They were rarely dispossessed from places assigned to them on the lands of the Arii and Raatira. Often they were able, if war did not shake up the society, to transmit the use of the land to their children. The Manahune usually enjoyed the fruits of their labor, making only such gifts as any inferior would give to a superior. A Manahune might become an Arioi (a member of the society of entertainers connected with the temples) or a priest. Usually his position as a priest would be proportionately inferior, but under certain conditions it might be superior even to that of the class above him. He might also profit from becoming a royal servant (de Bovis, 10, p. 22).

Scherzer (54, p. 247, footnote) calls the Manahune "tenantry at will." Wilson gives a similar impression. The vassalage of the Manahune, he says, "compels no constant service or residence: they may change chiefs, and go to another district . . . the meanest are in no slavish dependence. The honour and respect which they pay their chief, is rather through force of custom than the fear of punishment. They are admitted as their companions on all occasions, and treated with perfect freedom; indeed, in outward appearance they can hardly be distinguished. The king is not averse to converse with the lowest of his subjects, or to be their visitor; and never treats them with hauteur. His retinue is often changing; no man serves him longer than he pleases. They have no wages, nor engage for any stated time, though some remain in the same family all their lives . . ." (78, pp. 333-334). The lowest class received only the barest necessities and existed on a vegetable fare supplemented by shellfish, the remains of feasts, and what the chief shared with them of surplus fruit and fish. Forster mentions a chief sharing booty with the Teuteu (28, pp. 355-356, 370).

In pre-European times, once a Manahune, nearly always a Manahune. He might rise into the Raatira by some outright gift, but that would be rare (de

Bovis, 10, p. 22). In European times, however, the Manahune gradually managed to obscure their plebeian origin and improve their status. The plebeian class declined in the historic period because many moved socially upward into the Raatira class (Ellis, 21, vol. 3, p. 96; Henry, 36, p. 230). The population maladjustment following European settlement gave ambitious Manahune opportunities to occupy abandoned farms or to take uncultivated land. Today it would be impossible to single out particular individuals as descendants of the Manahune, because the class "has been so thoroughly assimilated into the great composite of Christianized native Tahiti, in which class distinctions are practically obliterated . . ." (Handy, 34, p. 8).

Henry and Ellis differ as to which class was the most numerous in the early days. According to Ellis (21, vol. 3, p. 96), the gentry always made up the bulk of the population; whereas Henry states (36, p. 230) that the Manahune greatly outnumbered the other classes until European times, when they merged with the middle class. The Arii were never numerous, but were, of course, influential.

Were the Manahune of the Society Islands a race of dwarfs like the Hawaiian Menehune? Handy's Tahitian informant (34, pp. 10, 44) was amused at the description of the Hawaiian Menehune. The Manahune of the Society Islands were "low in the social scale, but not low in stature." They were, this informant continued, indistinguishable from other Tahitians in stature or color, except when affected by differences in diet and exposure to the sun.

However, before the time of European settlement and the accompanying breakdown of native class structure, contrasts in stature and color between the social classes which resulted from differences in diet, exposure to the sun, selective breeding, and mode of life were pronounced enough for early European visitors to wonder if the population of the Society Islands were not composed of two distinct races. It was suggested that the race which was taller, fairer, and better built had perhaps achieved their dominant political position by conquering a shorter, darker, and less well-proportioned race of aborigines and relegating them to a plebeian status.

Both Forster (28, pp. 229, 263-264, 358-359) and Bougainville (9, pp. 251-252) who suggest the possibility of there being two distinct races add, however, that occasional members of the Manahune and of the Arii classes were exceptions to usual descriptions of the physical types of their classes. Forster, although inclining toward distinguishing two races in the population, emphasizes class differences in diet and conditions of life as factors in producing differences in appearance, which were more noticeable in the Society Islands than in the Marquesas or the Tongan Archipelago. In the Marquesas, he writes, no kind of food was overabundant and animal food was particularly rare. In the Tongan Islands, abundant vegetable and animal food, enough for all classes, resulted in less disparity in size between the ruling and the subject classes. In the Society Islands, the disparity was great, for only men of the ruling class could eat pork and dog; others had vegetable fare and were lucky to get shell-fish and blubber. Exposure to the sun and heavy, dirty work, according to Forster, made the lower ranks of both the Society and Tongan population thin and slender with solid, hard bones. The result was, he says (28, pp. 229-230, 263-264, 266, 358-359), that the lower class people "degenerate as it were towards the second race, but always preserve some remains of their original type; which in their chiefs . . . and the better sort of people, appears in its full luster and perfection."

Ellis (21, vol. 1, pp. 82-84), rejecting the supposition that two races were present in the Society Islands, feels that "different treatment in infancy, superior and more regular diet, bathing, distinct habits of life, and the relation that often prevails between the physical character of parents and their children, are sufficient" to account for the differences in appearance.

In the Society Archipelago, as in some other parts of Polynesia, royal children were secluded to keep their skin fair and to fatten them. Adults of the upper classes continued these beauty practices; but men seemed less inclined than women to bleach their skins, for a dark-skinned man, Ellis writes, was regarded as a strong man, perhaps because the sun-burned plebeians were so muscular. Class inbreeding, or rather the destruction of infants born of parents of unequal social status, also fostered the development of class differences in appearance.

In Maupiti Island, it is said, the terms Manahune and Raatira were "practically synonymous, signifying land-owning commoners," and the Manahune class was collectively known as the Hui Raatira or Taata Rii, little fellows (Handy, 34, p. 102). This puzzling and unexplained statement appears to identify the Raatira with the Manahune and to label both as little fellows, a term which might refer to physical condition or might connote comparative social insignificance. Presumably, this Manahune-Raatira class was set off from the Arii as in Raiatea, where, it is said, the terms Raatira and Mataeinaa (land divisions) were synonymous with Manahune, and all who were not Arii were Manahune (Handy, 34, p. 90).

As far as the physical type of the southern Manahune is concerned, it is certain that they were not a race of dwarfs. However, the kind of food they received and the life they led stunted their physical development and darkened their skins so that most of them were shorter and darker than the upper classes and appeared to some early European observers to have been a race apart. In Maupiti Island, class differences in appearance between the rulers and all others were marked enough perhaps to earn the commoners the descriptive name of "little fellows." Handy's statement on Maupiti quoted above is so ambiguous, however, that one hesitates even to try to fit it into the picture.

TUAMOTUAN USE OF THE TERM MANAHUNE

Emory tells me that he learned from an elderly Tuamotuan of Anaa Island that during the historic period the western Tuamotuans called anyone from the Society Islands a Manahune and applied the term without reproach or derogatory intent. In Raroia Island, according to an old manuscript Emory was given by a Tuamotuan in 1927, the chief named Maruake called together for the consecration of the chief named Varoa Tikaroa, groups of people which included the Marama, the Manahune, the Tanurepo (Dirt-Planters), the Vahitu (western Tuamotuan people), the Tapahuoe Tautua and the Tapahuoe Tauaro (central Tuamotus), and the Taravaia (Reao Island people). Also invited were groups of gods. In Faaiti Island, Emory was told that the term Manahune was applied only to the people of Tahiti and Moorea, whereas residents of Raiatea and others of the leeward islands were called the Marama. According to Handy (34, p. 81), the name of Marama is very distinguished and belongs to four related Arii families on Moorea, Huahine, Borabora, and Tahiti. The Manahune were regarded as non-raiders, whereas the Marama were feared as raiders.

According to other Tuamotuan information, Tatakoto and Vahitahi Islands, where Tahitians were called Manahune, regarded them as giants. But the Tatakoto view of them as friendly giants is not shared by other eastern Tuamotuans, according to Beckwith (5, p. 334), who quotes from a manuscript by J. F. Stimson.

MANAHUNE AS AN EPITHET

Linked with the Tuamotus is the use of the term Manahune as an epithet for an ancestor of the distinguished Pomare family of Tahiti (Handy, 34, p. 76; Adams, 1, p. 84). Taaroa-manahune was the son of Tu, a Tuamotuan from Fakarava Island, who was adopted into an Arii family of Tahiti. Otoo (O-Tu), mentioned by Captain Cook, was a descendant of Tu and Taaroa-Manahune. Because the Tahitians regarded the Tuamotuans as savages and social inferiors, the Pomares tried to hide their Tuamotuan connection and, it is said, an allusion to this heraldic blot might cost a man his life. It would be of interest to know, then, how the epithet of Manahune, which appears to refer to the lowly origin of this ancestor, came to be publicly attached to his son's name; but I can find no explanatory story of the particular circumstances.

Both Tahiti and Moorea were known formerly as Plebeian Tahiti. But this description is best known in connection with Tahiti, which was called Great Tahiti to distinguish it from Moorea, or Little Tahiti. The epithet of Manahune was applied to Tahiti, according to Henry (36, p. 230), because the population was formerly composed of democratic people ruled by warrior chiefs. "Later on came branches of the highest royal family of Opoa in Ra'iatea, who by marriage became rulers of the people in their respective districts, until gradually all the land became subjugated to the dynasty of Pomare, the people of each class retaining possession of their hereditary lands."

Raiateans, replying to the boasting of Tahitians about Tahiti, call it Tahiti-nui-Manahune (Great-Manahune-Tahiti) or, as Henry translates it, Great Plebeian Tahiti. Raiateans claim Tahiti and Moorea as their fish, because Tahiti is described in a chant as having been a part of Havaii, the old name of Raiatea, before it magically turned into a fish which tore itself loose from Raiatea and swam to a distance from it. The chant narrates that "there was no royal family (Hui Arii) upon Tahiti-of-the-warriors as it came away; the warriors who owned it and their clans took charge of the land as it broke loose; for this cause it was named Tahiti-manahune." (See Henry, 36, pp. 436-439.) Tahiti, the fish, had to have its sinews cut to keep it from moving, but the task was accomplished with difficulty, according to the chant, because Tahiti-mana-hune had no gods. However, the victorious warrior Tafai cut the sinews, and, to quote Henry's interpretation of the subsequent events, "warrior chiefs became warrior kings over plebeian Tahiti, and gradually their families intermarried and became one with the royal family of Opoa in the motherland," Raiatea (36, pp. 443-445).

The coming of the gods to Moorea and Tahiti from Havaii is next described in the chant. The north winds carried the gods who came by the tens and the thousands to southern Tahiti, where they frightened the people into caves and ravines. Later the gods dispersed through the island and the people returned to their valleys. The gods, the chant states, demanded the heads of warriors for their temples. Taaroa, Tu, and Tane (to the latter of whom Taaroa gave great power) were the principal gods at the time, according to a statement that follows the chant but does not seem to be a part of it.

MANAHUNE AS ABORIGINES OF THE SOCIETY ISLANDS

Emory, it will be remembered from the summary of the research on the Necker and Nihoa cultures in the northern Hawaiian Islands, spoke of the Manahune as the aboriginal settlers of the Society Islands who had a culture like that of the Necker-Nihoa residents. Handy and Buck are two other present-day anthropologists who regard the Manahune as the descendants of the original inhabitants of the Society Islands who were reduced to a low social position by conquering invaders. They differ, however, as to who the conquerors were and as to the relationship of the culture of the conquerors to that of the Manahune. According to Handy (34, pp. 3, 5, 43, 44; 35), who uses Tahiti as the focal point of his hypothesis, the culture in that island at the time of discovery was the result of the blending of two distinct cultural strata, the Old Tahitian and the Hui Arii. Each stratum, according to him, is associated with a distinct racial type and a distinct linguistic grouping. He believes that the Arii were a maritime, fishing people who lived on the shore and traced their descent from the god Taaroa and that the Old Tahitians lived in the interior, were agricultural, and worshiped Tane, Tu, and Roo. Many of the Old Tahitian culture elements, according to Handy's theory, entered Polynesia from Malaysia via Melanesia, while certain elements of the Hui Arii culture were "distinctively Micronesian" rather than Melanesian.

Handy says that the earlier stratum, the Old Tahitian, was that of the indigenous population, the ancestors of the serfs historically termed the Manahune. The later stratum, he continues, was that of the Hui Arii, a dynasty which came to Raiatea in the late sixth or early seventh century A. D. and subsequently conquered the Tahitian aborigines. Those of the vanquished people who were not killed or did not escape to other islands "remained in Tahiti to play an honorable role under the new regime," or became the servile class familiar from historic Tahiti. The Manahune of the historic period, Handy states, were "the subjugated and unassimilated bulk of the pre-*arii* population of 'plebeian Tahiti.' "

Variants of this so-called two-strata theory that Polynesian culture of the historic period was a fusion of two or more distinct cultures coming into Polynesia at different times from outside the area have been advanced by Stimson, Rivers, Williamson, Linton, Churchill, and, most extensively in mythology, by Dixon.

Piddington and Buck, who have critically examined the theory, advance a counter hypothesis that variations in Polynesian culture have arisen from a single culture as the result of a number of cultural processes such as inter-island diffusion, local efflorescence, adaptation, loss of elements, and substitution of materials. They do not deny that warfare between the islands was accompanied by invasion, conquest, and subjugation of the residents, but they object to the theory that a group of people with a different culture came from outside Polynesia and conquered and imposed their culture upon the first settlers of Polynesia.

As one of the "recorded instances of successful invasion" of one Polynesian people by another, Piddington (77, p. 226) mentions the Raiatean conquest of Tahiti. The Tahitian Manahune, he believes, were an accumulation of people who had been conquered in successive inter-island wars and had escaped to the hills while their conquerors took the more desirable land along the shore and reduced the refugees to a menial position. Geographic and demographic conditions in Tahiti, Piddington states, favor this tendency and the establishing of a "permanent type of local and social organization," meaning, I believe, the hierarchical class structure with the Arii and the Manahune living at different altitudes, literally.

Buck writes (15, pp. 475, 477, 516, 517), "Tahitian traditions term the earliest inhabitants of the Society Islands Manahune, and they are held to have had a simpler culture than that which developed later. The native historians naturally belong to a later period, and I believe that their story merely records an early stage in their own history." These earliest inhabitants entered Polynesia, Buck believes, by way of Micronesia. Expeditions from the Society Islands, where some of them settled, later went to New Zealand, where they came to be known as Tangata Whenua (People of the Land), and to Hawaii, where they were called Menehune, a term related to that for the Society Island settlers. Traditions, Buck continues, describe the Manahune, the Menehune, and the Tangata Whenua as lacking domestic animals and cultivable food plants and depending on food gathering and fishing. In this connection, he mentions that Hawaiian fishponds, generally credited to the Menehune, are indicative of Menehune dependence on fish. As to this latter point, it will be recalled that stories do not mention the Menehune using the ponds themselves. They merely built them for the Hawaiian chiefs.

Raiatea became the center of cultural development; and its higher culture, which Buck, like Handy, calls the Arii culture, spread through the Society Archipelago. Arii invaders from Raiatea conquered Tahiti; drove the Manahune, who still were in the earlier cultural stage, to the interior; and made them their serfs and farmers. About the thirteenth century, Buck continues, the Raiatean cultural pattern was carried to the Cook Islands and to Hawaii where it replaced the culture pattern "of the earlier Menehune, who were absorbed by the newcomers." That older cultural pattern survived for a time on Necker and Nihoa Islands. About a century later it reached New Zealand and replaced the Tangata Whenua culture.

As far as these hypotheses by Handy, Piddington, and Buck bear on the question of the identity of the Menehune and the Manahune, the two significant points to examine and find evidence for are (1) the use of the term Manahune as the name of the aborigines of the Society Islands and (2) the conquest and the subjugation of the Manahune by the Arii, particularly the conquest of the Tahitian Manahune by the Raiatean Arii.

Handy, it should be noted, tends to avoid using the term Manahune as the name of the aborigines; instead, he refers to the aborigines as the ancestors of the Manahune and states that he intends to refer to them as the *maori,* meaning indigenous (35, p. 8). He reserves the term Manahune for their assumed descendants, the people who formed the lowest social class in historic times.

Traditions are mentioned by the above-named ethnologists as constituting their major source of evidence for the two points listed above. What these traditions are on which they build this complex superstructure, I have found it hard to discover. The chants and information discussed in the previous section about the Manahune as a social class and the use of the word as an epithet for

Tahiti and Moorea represent all that I have been able to find. One of these chants, which is from Tahiti, orders the Manahune, the slaves of the Arii, to go to the mountains where they belong. The other, it will be recalled, is the long chant which tells of the separation of Tahiti (as a fish) from Raiatea; the severing of the sinews of the fish; the absence of a chiefly family, a Hui Arii, from Tahiti at this time when it had only warrior lords and so was called Tahiti-Manahune; and the arrival of the gods on Tahiti which frightened the people.

Handy (35, p. 16) and Buck accept the latter chant, which uses the customary figurative and metaphorical style of Polynesian narrators, as a traditional but reliable account of the history of the Raiatean conquest of Tahiti. Apparently, it is also accepted as trustworthy evidence by Piddington, who writes, without giving his source, of the conquest of Tahiti by Raiatea as an example of a recorded instance of successful invasion (77, p. 266). This is in spite of his later statement that because the content of fact in Polynesian oral traditions is fragmentary and the events are far away in time with many chances for distortions to occur, "their claims to historical authenticity can hardly be admitted as possessing *prima facie* validity."

It seems to me, after examining the chant which constitutes the sole basis for the claim that the Manahune are the aborigines of not only Tahiti but of all the Society Archipelago, that the situation is almost as confused and indeterminate as in the identification of the Hawaiian Menehune as the aborigines of northern Polynesia. The only bit of evidence offered to justify the use of the term Manahune as synonymous with aborigine is in the chant which refers to Tahiti as Tahiti-manahune because it had warrior lords but no Arii until the Arii of Havaii (Raiatea) established themselves there through conquest.

It strikes me that the obvious interpretation of the epithet in this context is in terms of existing class distinctions from the viewpoint of the Arii of Havaii who regarded themselves as socially superior to any and all Tahitians. In the chant, they justify their conquest of Tahiti on the grounds that, as both Tahiti and Moorea were physically parts of Raiatea until magically separated, the Arii were simply taking back what belonged to their island; also, to them, the Tahitians were heathens since they did not worship the same gods as the people of Havaii hence the latter were spreading the gospel to Tahiti; and finally, since Tahiti had no Arii class (Havaii did not consider the warrior lords Arii) and were just a bunch of commoners (Manahune), the people of Havaii were going to elevate the social status of Tahiti by giving them royalty. The Tahitians evidently resisted this uplift until the tide turned and they were forced to flee to the hills to hide. The only way that I can see to interpret Tahiti-manahune as Tahiti-the-aboriginal rather than Tahiti-plebeian is to look at it from the standpoint of the Havaii Arii. It is a matter of comparison. To the Arii of

Havaii and their war parties who settled on Tahiti, the Tahitian Manahune were the aborigines of Tahiti. They ignored any class distinctions Tahitians might have drawn between the warrior lords of their own land and the followers of these lords, and called them all Manahune.

If one is going to interpret the Manahune as aborigines and extend that interpretation to all of the Society Islands from reading this meaning into the poetically phrased Tahitian chant, then one must conclude, unless the two-strata theory of Handy is invoked, that the Arii also are Manahune in the sense of being aborigines who have set themselves on the top rung of the social ladder they built and have taken a new name, leaving the term Manahune for their lower class kinsmen. But there is no evidence that Society Islanders ever interpreted Manahune as aborigines or as anything other than a social class below the chiefs, the Arii.

Some of the conquered population of an island might suffer a decline in social status under their conquerors. For instance, middle class members sometimes sank into the landless class; but, on the other hand, others rose in rank usually through marriage with the conquerors. Some of the Manahune lost out and escaped to the hills; others, perhaps, as in Christian times, took advantage of the disordered society to improve their social status.

Those Tuamotuans who called the people of Tahiti and Moorea Manahune declared that they were not feared because they were not invaders like the Marama, people of the leeward islands. The Tuamotuans appear to have adopted the terminology of the chant which identified all Tahitians as Manahune, a classification apparently of the people of Havaii, among whom the Marama was a leading Arii clan.

The connotation of the name Manahune with plebeian status, even when used as a personal name, as in the case of Taaroa-manahune, is persistent. Although one people is legendary and the other a verifiable reality into historical times, the Hawaiian Menehune and the Society Manahune share, in addition to their common name, the role of plebeian workers. The Menehune, however, specialize in stone work and a little canoe-building, whereas the Manahune are laborers, not craftsmen. Both the Menehune and the Manahune customarily reside in the interior of islands. Both are regarded as physically smaller than the class employing them, although the Society Manahune are far from being dwarfs like the Menehune. And, to the Tuamotuans, the Manahune are giants.

Other comparisons, such as the limited diet, might be drawn, but these comparisons are rather tenuous. The simple culture attributed to the Hawaiian Menehune, to the Tahitian Manahune, and to the odd bands elsewhere in Oceania which I will discuss later, may represent merely the slum culture of the underprivileged, a culture which existed side by side with the more comfortable life of the upper class. The simple culture described rather idealistically as if it were a past Golden Age, which is the storyteller's privilege, does not necessarily represent a survival of a more primitive life. It may be only a washed-out form of the current culture. War refugees, or wild men, would lead a similarly simple life, supplementing it with what they could steal at night from the lowland settlers. When the name Manahune was introduced into Hawaii, it probably carried with it the idea of a plebeian, mountain-dwelling workman who was inferior, psychologically, physically, and socially to the class employing him.

The survey of the Tahitian data about the Manahune suggests that the name and its application to a laboring class probably diffused from central Polynesia to the Hawaiian Islands, where, if it ever was applied to the laboring class as in the south, it was long ago replaced by the term Makaainana. The fact that the dialectical variation has developed suggests that the name of the southern Manahune has been present long enough in the north to be altered to Menehune. Finally, before the survey continues to other islands, it may be noted that there is no evidence of sufficient weight to justify regarding either the Menehune or the Manahune as the first settlers of their islands.

THE MANAUNE IN THE COOK ISLANDS

Manaune is the Cook Islands dialectical equivalent of Menehune and Manahune. The term occurs in Rarotonga, where it is applied to one of Chief Tangiia's bands of followers, and in Mangaia, where it is the name of a politically prominent tribe which traces its descent from an eponymous ancestor, Manaune. Buck has a reconstruction of the history of the Mangaians which involves the assumption that they were plebeians from Rarotonga who tried, in Mangaia, to hide their lowly origin. The names of Tangiia's bands and the occurrence of the name Manaune in Mangaia are important in the reconstruction.

Three different lists name bands of people associated with Tangiia, a Tahitian who settled on Rarotonga after much trouble resulting from his jealousy over the privileges of his cousin, who outranked him. Two of the lists share seven names, eight if Te Kopa is an abbreviated, misspelled form of Te Kapatavarivari. The first of these lists names eight bands that fought for Tangiia on Tahiti; the second list names nine bands placed by Tangiia under the chieftainship of his adopted son. Manaune is the name of the ninth band on the second list (Tara-Are, 57, pp. 187, 200), and the only one absent from the first list (57, pp. 194, 206), except for the doubtful one mentioned.

The third list, of Rarotongan origin like the first two, names the eight bands in Tangiia's canoe, an unexplained statement which may refer to the people who accompanied the chief to Rarotonga from Tahiti (Buck, 12, p. 31). Of the eight names, only four appear on the other two lists. Manaune does not appear on this third list. In other words, Manaune appears on only one of the three lists naming Tangiia's bands of people.

The following chart gives the names of Tangiia's bands. I have rearranged the sequences to show first the similarities existing among the three lists.

Warrior Bands	Adopted Son's Bands	Canoe Bands
1. Te Neke	1. Te Neke	1. Te Ne'epoto
2. Te Kakipoto	2. Te Kakipoto	2. Te Kakipoto
3. Te Ataataapua	3. Te Ataatapua	3. Te Ataatapua
4. Te Tataveremoepapa	4. Te Tataveremoepapa	4. Te Tatavere
5. Te Tavakemoerangi	5. Te Tavakemoerangi	5. Te Vakevake
6. Te Atutakapoto	6. Te Atutakapoto	6. Te Raetiki
7. Te Tavakeoraurau	7. Te Tavakeoraurau	7. Te Kairira (Kairia)
8. Te Kopa	8. Te Kapatavarivari	8. Te Mangaia
	9. Te Manaune	

The Mangaian myths and traditions are unorthodox for Polynesians, Buck points out, because (1) the first human settlers are described as appearing abruptly from the underworld to colonize Mangaia, (2) a prominent line of chiefs who inherited the religious authority of the island is given an immediate divine origin, and (3) other genealogical lines between the period of divine origin and human settlement are also comparatively brief. Buck's interpretation is that the Mangaians were plebeians who tried to hide their humble ancestry by omitting the names of relatives who should, in an orthodox genealogy, intervene between the gods and the colonists. Though betraying tampering, the genealogies based on this technique did enable Mangaians to ignore Rarotonga, the island whence they came, and their lowly relatives and to throw in an insult at Rarotonga by debasing its principal god.

One of the bands occupying Tangiia's canoe was called Mangaia, a name absent from the other two lists. According to Buck (12, p. 32), the name Manaune on the adopted son's, or second, list is a substitute for the name Mangaia. He apparently regards the Mangaia and the Manaune bands as identical. He suggests that Tangiia supplemented his company with recruits from the Manahune, "the older inhabitants of Tahiti." While the other Tahitian bands accompanying him gained hereditary honors as Tangiia's star brightened in Rarotonga, "the Mangaia or Manaune groups had no chance of rising in the social scale." When these submerged people moved to Mangaia to start a new life, they expressed their antagonism to Rarotonga and concealed their origins (or so they hoped) by reorganizing their traditions and genealogies.

The use of Manaune as a personal name for a fairly recent Mangaian ancestor whose tribe, named after him, won the temporal power of Mangaia through warfare, indicates, according to Buck (12, pp. 33, 76-80), "some memory of an ancestral use of the name," and "the association of Mangaia with the older Polynesians." The Mangaian use of the term Manaune does not refer, Buck emphasizes, to an early wave of settlement or to a grade of society as in Tahiti and Hawaii.

With regard to equating the names Manaune and Mangaia on the lists of Tangiia's bands, it should be pointed out that logically the Manaune band could be equated with any of the other seven bands on the canoe list. Similarly the Mangaia band could be identified with any of the other eight bands on the adopted son's list, as with the ninth band, the Manaune. Treating the Mangaia and Manaune bands as one band under different names fits so neatly and comfortably into the reconstruction of Mangaian history and the explanation for its unorthodox mythological pattern that it is easy to ignore the other logical possibilities. That the Manaune, a tribe given by Tangiia to his adopted son, was a band of commoners is based on inference from the fact that Tangiia came from Tahiti, where the Manahune, a people with a name related to that of the Manaune, were plebeians. The Manahune are not among the eight bands of people he brought from Tahiti, however. That the Manaune band is the same as the Mangaia band on a Rarotongan list seems to me difficult to prove. Logically any of the other names not repeated on the lists might be equally interchangeable. The theory that the Mangaians were plebeians, or Manahune, in their homeland is better supported by evidence that they juggled their genealogies and traditional history, presumably to obscure their humble origins, than by the interpretation of the names of the two bands (Manaune and Mangaia) as synonyms.

It may be of interest to emphasize, incidentally, what an honorable name Manaune became in Mangaia because of the glory of the tribe and of individuals bearing the name. The Manaune tribe won for itself not only the position of temporal lord of the island but a goodly share of the land. The eponymous ancestor, Manaune, was adopted as a boy into the clan of his mother's nephew and grew up to fight against his father's kin, for which the gods punished him with insanity until he made atonement to them. Gill (30, pp. 136-140, 166-171) writes that in the course of time, there originated "one of the principal warrior tribes of Mangaia, named after the founder Manaune, and possessing now about half the soil of the island." Chief Manaune is associated in traditions with Rori, a "wild man," a war refugee, who, it is said, lived for 30 years in the wilderness, until succored by Manaune. Rori was a craftsman who made for Manaune a carving of Tiaio, the shark god worshiped by the people of the tribe. He later carved many other Mangaian gods, which are now in the London Missionary Society Museum. Rori taught younger men to carve, to plait sennit, to manufacture adzes, to build houses, and to work in stone. The refrain of a long, popular song telling how Rori was saved refers figuratively to Chief Manaune as a rock. A verse follows:

> Kindly succored by a friend,
> On the lands of Manaune,
> Rori reared up a family.
> Oh for a rock under whose shadow I might rest!

With this verse, we may conclude the information from east-central Polynesia relative to the names which are dialectically related to the Hawaiian Menehune.

NEW ZEALAND AND THE MENEHUNE

In notes inserted into articles in the Journals of the Polynesian Society from 1919 to 1921, the editor refers to the traditional acquaintance of Maori of New Zealand with a people called Manahua, a term which he uses synonymously with Manaune, Manahune, and Menehune. In Maori, he states, the word means a scar or cicatrice "such as the Melanesians mark their bodies with." (See 50, vol. 28, p. 194; vol. 29, pp. 72-73; 51, vol. 30, pp. 81-82.)

Elsdon Best (7, p. 16) lists Te Tini-o-Te-Makahua (The Multitude-of-the-Makahua) as one of the North Island tribes or subtribes tracing their descent from Toi, who is regarded as having settled in New Zealand before the coming of the fleet of colonists who arrived in the mid-fourteenth century, A.D. Subsequently, Best gives a version of the myth about the heroic Tawhaki (7, pp. 911-916), in which appear Te Tini-o-Te-Manahua, a term that Best adds parenthetically is "sometimes given as Makahua." They first slay Tawhaki, who is magically restored to life, then kill his father. Tawhaki and his brother eventually slay the multitude of the Manahua with the aid of a flock of dogs from heaven. It is not clear whether Best regards Makahua and Manahua as dialectical variants or as two different companies of spirits playing a similar role in different versions of the Tawhaki myth. Tawhaki also destroys the Ponaturi, the people of Tangaroa (god of the ocean) by trapping them in the house to which they come each night, then letting the sun shine on them.

It is for the linguists to decide whether the term Manahua is a dialectical variant of Manaune, Manahune, and Menehune.

The assumed Melanesian connection of the Manahua, which is implied in the meaning of the word as interpreted by the editor, also occurs in his references to the Menehune. He regards the Hawaiian and Tahitian people with the related names as non-Polynesian in physical type. Descriptions of the Hawaiian Menehune suggest to him that they might be either Negrito or Melanesian people, more likely Negrito, "for Hawaiians have apparently had little to do with Melanesia." He adds that the Menehune might be "some of the negroid people of Indonesia brought into the Pacific by the ancestors of the Polynesians to man their canoes." The Negrito element is introduced into the discussion because of Dixon's theory that a Negrito element exists in Polynesia in only the Hawaiian Islands, where it is concentrated in Kauai. (See 50, vol. 29, p. 72; vol. 30, pp. 80-81.)

Henry is quoted by the editor as stating that the Tahitian Manahune were a small people (a reference I am unable to locate in Henry's writing), who 38 generations past had a chief named Taaroa-manahune. (The origin of the epithet Manahune for Chief Taaroa was discussed above.) The editor (51, pp. 80-81) refers to some of Tangiia's bands being made up of little people, but I am unable to find confirmation in any accounts about Tangiia. He perhaps interpreted the Manahune band in Tangiia's canoe as being dwarfs like the Menehune of Hawaiian folklore.

To the editor's suggestion (51, pp. 82, 262) "that the Tongan people were acquainted with the Manahune under the name Haa-Meneuli," Collocott replies that he can find no confirmation of the idea.

F. W. Christian informed the editor that the Manaune of Mangaia "are stated by Taniera, their chief, to have come originally to Mangaia from Rapanui or Easter Island, and that in appearance they resemble the people of the Tokerau Islands." The editor remarks that "if they did come from Easter Island, this furnishes a *very* slight link, with some carvings depicted by Mrs. Scoresby Routledge in her 'The Mystery of Easter Island,' which carvings are supposed to be Melanesian, as we suppose the Manahune to be Melanesians, but the evidence is by no means conclusive . . ." (51, p. 262).

MYTHOLOGICAL CHARACTERS REMINISCENT OF THE HAWAIIAN MENEHUNE

RECURRENT CHARACTERS AND BELIEFS

The Manahune known in the Society, Cook, and Tuamotuan Archipelagoes were definitely members of *Homo sapiens,* who unquestionably were visible to other human beings, whether Polynesians or Europeans, and whether they had supernatural or natural vision. Supernatural qualities sufficient to set them apart from their fellow Polynesians have not been attributed to the central Polynesian Manahune and Manaune. In this they contrast with the Hawaiian Menehune, with whom their most specific resemblance is in name. However, in this central region and in other parts of Polynesia, Micronesia, and Melanesia, there are mythological characters whose qualities and activities recall the Hawaiian Menehune, although they do not bear names dialectically related to that term. Several islands have myths about bands of people different from the rest of the population.

Elements in the sets of native beliefs about these bands recur in island after island. Below is a list of 22 recurrent beliefs.

1. They live in forests, mountains, and other isolated areas in the interior of a country.
2. They live only in certain localities in the interior.
3. They live in caves or underground.
4. They eat uncooked forest products and fish.
5. Often they are said to lack fire.
6. They are aborigines of the country who preceded the ancestors of the present native population.

7. They have almost entirely vanished since Europeans came, although a few remain.
8. They guard the forests and other natural resources and punish human beings who violate their tapus.
9. They are artisans: stoneworkers, canoe-builders, or island-builders.
10. They are active on the earth or around human beings only at night.
11. Being nocturnal toilers, they abandon any work unfinished at dawn.
12. They fear daylight, for it is dangerous to them. Daylight may be used to trap or kill them.
13. They are invisible to human beings except under certain circumstances.
14. Generally, they are benevolent toward human beings, but have their malevolent, capricious moments.
15. They have unusual supernatural abilities and can magically possess people and cause illness.
16. They are peculiarly noisy and talkative, speaking a strange chatter.
17. Often they are sweet singers, however, and like music.
18. They frequently have a reputation for thievishness and little tricks and jokes.
19. They are regarded by human beings as rather unpersonalized companies with marked social cohesion and a uniform character structure. Individuals rarely stand out or are named.
20. They are short in stature and sometimes different physically in other respects from other island residents whom they occasionally marry.
21. Some of them were magically transformed into stones, which are still pointed out.
22. Human beings in the area vacillate between fear and amusement with regard to them.

These are only some of the recurrent beliefs, and not all of them are associated with every band. Desirable as it would be to have a detailed study of all of these supernatural groups and the myths with related features, I shall only sample the material to show that the beliefs connected with the Hawaiian Menehune are not unique, but are a part of the mythological stock-in-trade of many neighboring Pacific islanders among whom the beliefs have diffused.

Bands of woodland spirits whom the natives regard as completely supernatural are common in Pacific mythology and share similarities with those bands believed to represent survivors of early residents. It will be recalled that the Eepa, the Mu, the Wa, the Wao, and the Menehune were sometimes difficult to distinguish from each other and were occasionally described as related tribes in the Hawaiian myths given earlier.

POLYNESIA

The name of Laka, the hero for whom the Menehune built and launched a canoe in the Hawaiian Islands, changes to Lata, Rata, Lasa, Ata, or Aka, in other parts of Polynesia and in Melanesia (Beckwith, 5, pp. 262-275). The episodes of raising the fallen tree and building the canoe, usually a part of the Laka myth, also occur independently of it in myths about other heroes. Those variants of this episode which are most closely related to the Hawaiian are found in the Marquesas, the Society Islands, the Cook Islands, the Tuamotus, and in New Zealand.

Companies of woodland spirits, birds, crabs, insects or combinations of these types assist the hero by magically building and launching his canoe after they have restored the sacred tree which he has chopped down in violation of the tapus of the god of the forests. Only in the Hawaiian Islands do the Menehune work for Laka. This indicates that it was in Hawaii that a narrator inserted the Menehune into the myth as a substitute for the woodland sprites in the other versions. Perhaps he did this because of the association of the Menehune with the forests, with rapid work, and with craftsmanship—qualities that they have acquired, for all we know, from the same mythological storehouse which Hawaiians share with other Polynesians and from which the woodland spirits are granted their talents too.

The Hawaiian Laka myth is not a local invention except for such details as the substitution of Menehune for other woodland characters. Unfortunately, the English translation of the Hawaiian version (Thrum, 62) was published in only a generalized form, so that detailed comparisons cannot be made with variants found elsewhere in Polynesia. One indication of the close historical connection of the Hawaiian version with the southern Polynesian myths is that in both regions two named spirits act as leaders to restore the fallen tree and later to build Laka's canoe. In Hawaii, as well as in Tahiti, the Tuamotus, and the Marquesas, the hero seizes the two chief artisans and forces them to help him. In Tahiti and the Tuamotus, one of the two spirits is the chief of the band, while the other is the leading artisan. In Tahiti, as in Hawaii, Laka catches them after hiding under the fallen tree to spy on the spirits who more than once have set up the tree he has chopped down. In both islands, the spirits chant as they go to work, calling on the innumerable gods to help them undo the harm Laka has done in the forest.

The southern elves, like the Menehune, are invisible except to their friends. The Tuamotuan spirits are odd, merry little beings, some stout, others slender. Toahiti-of-the-jovial-face, their leader, is the god of every deep valley. In New Zealand, the little people of Tane, the forest god, are personified insects and birds, who erect the tree chopped down by Rata and build his canoe.

Like the Menehune, Toahiti's elves and the artisan birds in the Aitutaki (Cook Islands) version, build Laka's canoe in one night. In Tahiti, it takes a day and half a night, a most unusual work shift for Polynesian spirits, who usually toil only after dark. In Mangaia, for instance, people feed their gods before sunset to enable the eager gods to start their tour of the island, which they do only at night. "Ashamed" of daylight, they rush back at dawn with a great noise. (See Gill, 30, p. 333.)

In New Zealand, the Ponaturi are a keen-nosed band of spirits who live in the ocean by day and on earth by night. Tawhaki traps them and other mythical bands by stuffing chinks of the house with garments to keep them sleeping after dawn. Exposure to the sun kills them, as it does a shy, forest-dwelling band in the Chathams, the Tangaro-Motupua (Grey, 32, pp. 43-47; Shand, 55, pp. 126-127).

The heroic Maui's parents, like other supernatural beings, often live on the earth by night and leave before dawn for the underworld, where their gardens are located. Maui uses the chink-stuffing trick to delay his mother so that he can follow her at dawn (Grey, 32, p. 15).

Four western Polynesian islands—Futuna, Pukapuka, Uvea, and Niue— and the Society Islands in central Polynesia explain the location or character- istics of the landscape of certain islands as the result of daylight coming natu- rally or by artificial inducement before nocturnal-working spirits have finished their work. Futuna Island has valleys and precipices because daylight came before Maui, the earth-fisher, could flatten out the island (Burrows, 16, p. 26). According to Niueans, Samoan spirits stole an island but dropped it at sunrise (48, p. 117). In Pukapuka and Uvea, the nocturnal-working spirits did not finish their task because daylight was made to come earlier than usual. An Uvean spirit, who, like the Samoan demons, was an island-stealer, stole some islands one night; but his sneezing woke up other spirits, one of whom imitated the sun and started a cock crowing. The thief dropped the islands where they now are (Burrows, 17, p. 162). Pukapukans explain that their island got its present size because Mataliki, who emerged from a stone which other gods were helping to grow into an island, did not want a large island; he caused dawn to come, and the gods fled, leaving the island small (Beagleholes, 2, pp. 375-377).

The myth from the Society Islands, given in French without the native text, states that Raiatean "genies" determined to steal beautiful Mount Rotui. On a dark night, two brothers and their sister looped a long cord around the moun- tain and slowly moved it. A good genie who saw them imitated the crow of a cock, thus leading the wicked three to believe that day was approaching. The two brothers were transformed into two great stones, the sister into a block of coral. But Mount Rotui, which formerly was in the interior of the country, is now at the seashore. (See Tefaafana, 58.)

A band sometimes compared with the Hawaiian Menehune is that of the Patupaiarehe, who live in the mountains and forests of certain parts of New Zealand. Many have disappeared, because fire has destroyed their homes and Europeans have invaded their land. They are regarded as a race of supernatural beings with supernatural powers, including invisibility. They go out only at night and on cloudy days. Maori use steam from cooking ovens and a mixture of shark oil and ochre to exorcise the Patu, who, though usually shy, benevo- lent, and peaceloving, have malicious moments. They slay or afflict people sleeping in their houses at night. The Patu get blamed, writes Best (7, pp. 994-1000), when people suffocate from lack of ventilation.

If attacked, the Patu defend themselves, although not too successfully. A Patu war party which was transformed into rocks is pointed out in one district; and earthworks of their fortified villages also exist. They protect the forests, guarding sacred places and preserving Maori land for the Maori. They carry off trespassers or violators of tapus, but usually release them unharmed after warning them. A disrespectful woman was captured by Patu, but was rescued by relatives who first used magic to put the Patu to sleep.

Opinions differ about Patu height. Some say that they are of ordinary stature; others call them little people. They have golden or reddish hair and blue or black eyes. A few Patu men have married Maori women, and cross-breeding, narrators claim, has produced the occasional albino seen among the Maori. The Patu men are devoted to their alien wives. One Patu chief, who brought his Maori wife home each morning and fetched her at night, was finally driven away with steam and the mixture of shark oil and ochre. Another Patu man, who secretly won the village virgin, was trapped by the chink-stuffing trick so that no dawn light entered the house and he overslept. He settled down in the Maori village, but later took the people to visit his home, where in the house of learning he taught his father-in-law certain secret knowledge not known to the Maori.

The Patu treasure anything red, especially their red flax garments, red pigs, and red eels. They live mostly on forest products and fish. For entertainment, they play the flute, the sweet sound of which is still heard at times.

New Zealand has many other bands of legendary forest protectors, who have not yet been mentioned. Te Tini-o-Te-Hakaturi, who guard the forests for Tane, restored Rata's tree and built his canoe. Other shy forest bands, sometimes regarded by Europeans and Maori as predecessors of the Maori, include the Keketoro, the Turehu, and the Tutumaiao (Best, 7, pp. 994-1000; White, 73, pp. 188-189; Cowan, 20, pp. 96-102, 142-151). The Maeroero, who do not seem to be a band, but scattered individuals, are wild, long-haired men who preserve natural resources and tell the people when they have enough flax or fish. The Maeroero are non-mortal, as bullets do not penetrate them (Beattie, 3, pp. 212-225).

MICRONESIA

Micronesia also has traditions about little people, according to F. W. Christian (18, pp. 110-115, 137, 382) and Paul Hambruch (33, vol. 7, pt. 1, pp. 366-367; pt. 3, pp. 99-102) who heard about them, under the name of Chokalai, on Ponape Island in the Carolines. Both visited a stone cemetery believed to have been their burial place. In the Marshall Islands, the Nonieb and the Anjinmar are little bush people.

In 1896, Ponapeans told Christian that the Chokalai, as they call the little folk, occupied the island before the coming of the Kona, who were giants, and the Liot, who were cannibals. Ponapeans described the Chokalai as dark-skinned, flat-nosed dwarfs who lived in the depths of the forest, where they chattered and gibbered like bats. Because they are still believed to haunt the forests, Ponapeans avoid the wooded areas, for the Chokalai are revengeful and malignant. They once killed a man who invaded their dell to plant kava.

Ponapeans say that the people now living at the mouth of the Palang River are descendants of the Chokalai, for they are thieving and treacherous, their speech has a "most foolish undercurrent of chatter," and they are shorter and darker than their neighbors. Like the Chokalai, the Palang dwellers have flat noses. Their neighbors call them "Paikop-faces" because they look like the Paikop, the "most ill-favoured of fishes, with wide goggle-eyes, and a face as flat as a dish."

Although Ponape has many ruins of stone structures, only one, a cemetery, is associated with the Chokalai, who are believed to have made and used it. In remote Ponial Dell, in the south-central interior of the island, Christian saw this cemetery which is in the form of "an irregular or broken parallelogram," surrounded by a breastwork of stones. Christian's plate facing page 112 (18) shows a diagram of the cemetery of the dwarfs. In the cemetery are nine small vaults, three of which are on a platform five feet above the ground. These vaults are said to be Chokalai graves. Each vault is four or four and a half feet long and is roofed with large basalt slabs. Christian, who removed the slabs to investigate the interiors of the vaults, found only a diminutive stone gouge, a stone knife, and "a few pieces of mouldering bones," none of which is described. To Christian, the absence of red or white shell beads, which are common in certain other Ponapean stone vaults, indicated the antiquity of the Chokalai vaults. His Ponapean companions concluded that the Chokalai were "either very stupid people who wouldn't work, or very poor and barbarous wretches not to have any treasures to bury." Ponapeans declare that the bow, which "nowadays . . . is entirely out of use," was a Chokalai weapon and "was made of *Katiu* or Ixora wood, the bowstring of the bark of the Hibiscus, the arrows of Hibiscus wood, or slips of Alek or reed-grass, tipped with the spine of the sting-ray."

Christian's theory is that the Chokalai, whom he likens to the Maori Patu-paiarehe and the pixies of the Old World, were really Negrito hill tribes, who were gradually exterminated by the Kona, whom he regards as Malayo-Polynesians, and by the Liot, whom he thinks were Melanesians from the south. Christian adds that the Ponapeans, like the Marquesans and other islanders, are afraid to go into the interior now because of the fairy foes there—"doubtless a recollection of early struggles of the Malayan races in Indonesia and their own islands with the dwarf aborigines of the mountain and the bush." There is no supporting evidence.

In 1910, Hambruch obtained information in Ponape about the Chokalai, whose name he spells either as Tsokelai or Zokelai. He also saw tombs attributed to the dwarfs, but it is not clear to me that the ruins he saw were the same as those described by Christian. Farther up from the cemetery, Christian saw another parallelogram of stone work enclosing tombs, but he does not specifically say that it also was a Chokalai cemetery. This remoter tomb seems to be the one Hambruch describes and attributes to the little people.

Hambruch obtained two traditions which describe the little people as small, mischievous, noisy, and thievish evil spirits, who came from a foreign land to settle in certain places on Ponape. One tradition has most of them leaving Ponape after having been punished for stealing yams; the other has them all moving to new settlements on the island. Another reason given for their up-rooting themselves was that the chief was angry with them because they made a terrific racket, singing, dancing, and banging their drums when they drank kava.

The more detailed of the two traditions obtained by Hambruch narrates that the Chokalai came from outside Ponape and settled in Kiti, a district in the southwestern part of the island. Their holy places, now called Pankatara by Ponapeans, were at Rentu village in Uono, a section of Kiti. Other settlements, made as the population increased, were Olopel, Nateuta, and a small place called Panupots.

Chokalai looked like men, the tradition continues, but were much smaller and shorter; their legs were beautifully tattooed; they had beautiful voices and shouted loudly when happy; and they lived under the earth. People walking on the ground above them could hear them drumming below.

While feasting at Olopel, they stole Sau Kisa's yams. This so angered the chief that he furiously pelted the dwarfs with stones. They were frightened and left one night to live elsewhere on Ponape. During their exodus they created a valley still to be seen. In Auak they formed a band which always sat undisturbed in the community house gallery with their backs to the king's wall, a most insulting gesture. Gradually they increased and spread over Ponape. They still loiter today around Pilap, but they crawl into the ground when it rains. They magically possess and make sick any men whom they encounter. To be cured, the individuals must be exorcised and given medicine.

The people to settle on Ponape after the Chokalai were, according to tradition, the giants, whose ruins and graves are still pointed out. Hambruch remarks that, as on Kusaie and on Truk, it is narrated in Ponape that light-skinned giant people (Kona) who ate men came from the south.

Hambruch, like Christian, regards the Chokalai as having perhaps been the aborigines of Ponape. He saw occasional individuals in Palikir who greatly differed from other Ponapeans in being short, dark, curly haired, and broad-faced, with strong prognathism and low foreheads. Eighty years ago, he states, there were people in Palan (Christian's Palang) who were short and very dark, with high, clear voices and masses of curly hair. They were regarded as survivors of the oldest inhabitants of Ponape. Like Christian, Hambruch mentions the Jokasch (Christian's Chokach, the district in which Palikir is located) as saying that their neighbors, the Palan people, had Paikop faces.

Guamanians have two stories of large stones being dropped on the reef in their present location because the carriers were surprised by the arrival of daylight (Thompson, 59, p. 62).

In the Marshall Islands, according to Erdland (25, p. 314), the Anjinmar (also called Nonieb) are good-natured but singularly small beings, male and female, who live in the thick brush or in bushy grass. Although one can hear them talking and laughing, one cannot talk with them. Frequently they marry ordinary women and delight them with all kinds of wonderful presents. A woman of Ujae atoll, who lived alone on Abeju Island, once saw a bush spirit, Lekennat, who came to her that night with wonderful tasting fish and a perfume which came from his body. The two lived happily together and had a son. When the woman divulged her secret to her friends, the spirit disappeared forever. A rather similar story is told of a woman on Jaluit, who profited from the fine foods and mat-plaiting secrets of her spouse. She too lost him when she betrayed their secret.

Marshallese, like other Micronesians, have stories of giants. The Rimogaio are giants who live on Kille and spend six months of the year sleeping.

I heard no stories of little people in Tabiteuea Island in the Gilberts when I was there in 1948, but there was a genre of stories about a certain clan in a northern village. According to the stories the members of this group were constantly engaged in silly, suicidal behavior. Individuals who were pointed out to me looked and behaved as normally as any other Tabiteuean, but for reasons unknown to anyone this particular group has become the butt of every comic story the island hears. Ponape also has a genre of stories called *umes,* or "crazy people," about certain clans. This genre is mentioned here, for it is reminiscent of the kind of stories told of the mythical Masi of Melanesia, who, unlike the Micronesian clans, are beginning to be described by narrators as a band of little people.

MELANESIA

Folk beliefs about bands of odd, rarely individualized people, who live in the bush, occur in Melanesia, particularly in the Solomons and the neighboring islands. In the vicinity of San Cristoval are bands reminiscent of the Hawaiian Menehune (Fox, 29, pp. 10, 40, 129, 134-147, 290, 334, 345-346, 369-370). Sharing many similarities are the companies of odd people called the Kakamora, Kakangora, Pwaronga, and Pwamora in coastal San Cristoval; Toku, Katu, Waitarohia, and other names in the interior of San Cristoval; Mola, Tutu-langi, and Mumulou in Guadalcanal; Mwasiu in Ulawa Island; Nopitu or Dembit in the Banks Islands; Tuki in the Buka Passage region; Dodore in

North Malaita; Mumu in South Malaita; and Sakusaku among the Mono-Alu. Some are small, others large; some have only one foot, one arm and one eye; some have long red hair; others have long finger nails for stabbing men or putting out their eyes.

Certain bands of woodland spirits have acquired similarities to these odd folk. For example, some of the descriptions of the woodland Adaro in San Cristoval are similar to descriptions of the Kakamora. Stories of odd little people continue to be told; and every so often someone claims to have caught or at least seen the footprints of a member of one of these peculiar little people. During 1950, the Pacific Islands Monthly had two articles about the Guadalcanal small people. It appears that the natives are always ready to tell a newly arrived European that there really are little people still living in their island.

The Kakamora, to describe members of one group, are small. Some accounts say that they are 6 inches tall; others that they are 3 or 4 feet tall; still other narrators put them at 4 feet 6 inches or 5 feet. Skin color varies from light to dark. The hair is straight and often quite long, reaching to below the shoulders or even to the knees. While the teeth are very small, the nails are long and sharp and make up for a lack of weapons. Most of the Kakamora are harmless, but they have been known to eat a man, their small persons apparently enclosing a hearty appetite.

Each Kakamora is as strong as three or four men. The people are tricky and, for fun, steal garden produce and ornaments, count the fingers and toes of sleeping Melanesians, and gossip about them in a language different from that of other people. Anything white frightens them. Firearms have driven most of them away, but when the government confiscated firearms, the Kakamora became bold enough to venture near the villages, where they were seen or their footprints and the remains of their food were found. Kakamora love to dance and sing and are fast runners. Although natives believe that the government has a bounty on Kakamora, they have been unable to catch them to get a reward. Kakamora live in limestone clefts or in holes in banyan trees and depend on the forests for their food, which they eat raw, for they have no fire, except what they steal to play with. They go naked and lack arts of any kind. Their name is said to mean "native or original fools."

The greatest Kakamora deed was to bind up securely, with slender creepers, the rock which supports San Cristoval, after others with stronger ropes had failed at the job. Any large stonework is ascribed either to the Kakamora-like people or to another band, the Masi, with whom they are sometimes confused. Kakamora are also confused occasionally with Adaro, malevolent woodland spirits who lack human qualities.

Fox relates three other stories of the Kakamora. One tells of a group of blind Kakamora who held a dance in which a human boy joined. He was killed when each Kakamora tied a wisp of grass around his waist to establish his identity as a Kakamora. Another story tells of a sulky boy who cried because his parents did not give him what he wanted. A Kakamora carried him off, but the boy managed, unknown to his captor, to cling to a tree, from which his parents rescued him. The Kakamora arrived home, magically opened the cave wall in which he lived and sat down to eat his catch, but his bundle was empty! The third story is of a man who caught a female Kakamora, shaved off her hair, and married her. While the two worked in the bush with the wife guarding the family money, the husband burned the field to clear it, which so frightened the little Kakamora that she ran away but was not so scared as to drop the money. However, her husband enticed her back later to his sugar-cane field and caught her in a trap where she died. He got his money bag back.

San Cristoval has, besides the Kakamora, some small blind people and some one-eyed and noseless folk who can walk right through trees or rocks using magic words to open and close them.

The Boiboi are little river people.

The Mola of Guadalcanal are small like the Kakamora and have long hair and very dark skins, and eat children, whom they stab with their long nails and put into large bags. They make stone circles, the central stone being round, and into this they go. Like some Kakamora, they have a queen, named Voro, whose daughter will succeed her. Fox suggests that the name Mola is linked with Kakamora.

The South Malaita Mumu are like the Kakamora, but the North Malaita Dodore are large people.

Two Dodore stories are told. One tells of a man who made himself a mat from the banyan belonging to the Dodore. To get the mat back, they carried him off while he was asleep; but when he woke up, they ran away. Another story tells how the Dodore bewitch people and make them foolish. If one loses something and then finds it again near where it had been laid, the mischief is known to have been done by a Dodore. One narrator wandered the forest in a state of amnesia after meeting a tall, red-haired Dodore. The narrator's friends found him and magically restored him to his senses, taking off the Dodore spell.

A myth about eight tiny Mumu with long hair says that they used to catch people to eat but were afraid of anything red. Once when about to catch a man, they saw the red hibiscus he wore and ran away. Later, they went to his house to find him because of the pleasant smell of the flower. The people inside saw the Mumu approaching; and when the little people peeked in, they were caught by the hair. Although the people tried to kill them, they were unsuccessful until a treacherous Mumu who was nearby said, "Their death is in their buttocks." The people then killed seven little Mumu, but the eighth got away.

Stories like these about the Kakamora and other odd people are also told in the Buka Passage area about the Tuki and their enemies, the Pinari, a white-skinned, long-legged people; and of the Sakusaku people, who are *nitu* (spirits) and bush elves among the Mono-Alu (Blackwood, 8, pp. 342, 541).

The Masi of Ulawa and San Cristoval are identical with the Rere-ni-Mesi of Saa Island and with the people of Morodo of North Mala (Fox, 29, pp. 345, 370; Ivens, 39, chapters 20 and 40). A race of fools, the Qaqae, is said to live in the Banks Islands and to behave like Masi (29, p. 355). Masi means stupid. Like the Tabiteuean group mentioned above, the Masi have a genius for doing everything wrong, for suicidal behavior, and for running away when there is no need to escape. They spear their own feet, thinking them eels; they dive for sunbeams and drown themselves; and they launch their canoes from steep cliffs. They are crude, non-agricultural, and inland dwellers. Natives think them real people. In North Mala, they live on Morodo Ridge, hence their local name People of Morodo. Places and stone objects connected with them and the Kakamora are still pointed out.

These friendly, peaceful, and slap-happy buffoons are believed by Fox (29, pp. 40, 142, 370) to have originally been artisan slaves, a conquered or subject people, whom their masters or conquerors required to build canoes and do stone work and other heavy labor. Their reputed descendants of today are the skilled craftsmen of the islands. According to Fox, both the Masi and the Kakamora represent the Melanesians' memories of either the early residents whom they found on these islands and conquered or the people who lived in the homeland whence the present Melanesians came. The Masi, the theory continues, became an artisan class serving the conquerors, and their descendants carried on the crafts. Ivens (39) does not agree with Fox (29, pp. 369-370) that the skilled workers of today are descendants of the legendary buffoons.

As stonework of forgotten origin is sometimes attributed to the Masi, sometimes to the Kakamora, we can assume that physical differences between the two bands are also obscured by the storytellers. It is not surprising then that Ivens should have heard that the Masi are little people like the Kakamora, whereas Fox heard that the Masi are people of ordinary height.

Another band of strange people is the Muumuu, the babbling, wild men of Guadalcanal, who have long hair and stumps for feet (Ivens, 39, pp. 415-416). They resemble the Gosile of North Mala (Ivens, 40, p. 304).

Codrington (19, p. 152) writes of "a lesser folk of dwarfs and trolls" in the Banks Islands and the New Hebrides. They are full of magical power but are "comparatively rude and easily deceived." Banks Islanders categorically call all spirits *vui*, a term applied not only to those supernatural spirits who are incorporeal, but also to those who can assume human form. Marawa, the companion of the great mythical hero, Qat, is one of these strange people who are smaller and darker than the natives and have long, straight hair. Although Qat and other mythical characters like Tagaro and his brothers are believed to have left the islands forever, Marawa and others like him are said to have remained.

A man once encountered a small, long-haired man and followed him up a river valley to a narrow gorge closed by a rock. When the spirit, who was Marawa, knocked on the rock, it opened and he entered followed by the human being. The man, who later was sent home by Marawa to raise money, taxed his neighbors for contributions for Marawa so that they might win the good will of the spirit as he had done.

Marawa plays the role assigned in Hawaii to the Menehune and in other Polynesian islands to forest spirits, in that he restores each night a tree which Qat has chopped down that day for a canoe. Although Marawa sometimes has the form of a spider, in this adventure he is a little old man with long white hair and lives in the ground. Qat, like Lata, hides and watches Marawa restore the fallen tree, chip by chip. As Marawa searches for the last chip, Qat catches him. To save his life, he promises Qat, as the forest spirits and Menehune promised Lata, to build his canoe. This he does, using for the job his long, strong fingernails, like those of the Kakamora. (Iron nails, when introduced, were called Marawa's fingernails.) Marawa and Qat become good friends, and Marawa often helps Qat escape from his malevolent brothers, once by letting Qat use his long white hair as a ladder! It is interesting to note Codrington's statement that a Santa Cruz hero named Lata who made man and animals is regarded by people there as the Banks Islanders regard Qat (Codrington, 19, pp. 159, 161, 167). Whether or not the name Qat is a dialectical variant of the name Lata I do not know.

Long-nailed, long-haired, wild men of the mountains are also known; one who was seen was "like a man with small legs; when spoken to he did not answer, and when struck he did not feel," according to Codrington (19, pp. 169-170). And, shades of the Menehune and the Mu, he was holding bananas in his hand!

The appearance of a mythical band called Nopitu is not described by Codrington (19, pp. 153-154), but at least some of the Nopitu are small, for a human woman can carry one on her back like a baby. One of these spirits can enter a woman's body and be born later as an ordinary child. A Nopitu, like the Micronesian Chokalai, can also possess a human being so that he dances wildly and money falls from his hair when he scratches his head. Nopitu favor people who make them gifts of little red yams.

According to Fox (29, p. 140), the Nopitu are of many kinds. Some (who are like the San Cristoval Boiboi) come from the waves, turn into men and bewitch people. Others live in caves and holes in the ground. They are very small, about 6 inches tall, with long hair and sharp fingernails, and love anything red, such as red yams and red coconuts. They love to dance and decorate themselves with fragrant flowers. They bewitch people to do them harm, whereas they help others, especially fair-skinned people, by giving them strings of money or the power to extract money from their hair.

A bishop once saw a Nopitu-possessed woman "make" money. As she rubbed her hands, good money fell to the ground. Others, like a man on Florida Island, picked gold sovereigns from his hair. Says Fox, ". . . the *nopitu* would seem to be the San Cristoval *kakamora* with the attributes of *vui* (spirits) added to them."

Rivers (53, vol. 2, pp. 428-429) states that the stone walls and earth mounds on Santa Maria in the Banks Islands are ascribed to an indigenous people called Malavui or Malatunium, who are traditionally described as having had little or no sense. In these respects, they were like the Masi. They lived in the bushes without houses, and worked under the direction of a few sensible, normal people who lived among them. Linton (43, p. 15) thinks that the names of these supposedly indigenous people of Santa Maria "bear at least a superficial resemblance to the Hawaiian term, menehune." The resemblance strikes me as extremely far-fetched.

The origin of the Fijian *nanga* or stone ceremonial structure is ascribed to two little black-skinned old men who came across the sea from the west and landed near Nandi (Thomson, 60, p. 149; Rivers, 53, p. 430). These two beings and their descendants, who practise the mysteries of the Nanga cult, have no apparent connection with two other types of traditional little people of Viti Levu, the Veli, or woodland fairies, and the Luveniwai, water sprites described by Thomson (60, pp. 169-171), Williams (75, pp. 237-240), Brewster (11, pp. 88-89, 222-232), and others.

Brewster suggests that there may have been a dwarf or pygmy aboriginal population in Fiji before the Melanesians arrived, as the Fijians maintain that "the forests and waste spaces [are] still inhabited by a dwarf or pygmy folk, visible only to the faithful handsome little folk with large fuzzy mops of hair. . . ." There is no supporting evidence for Brewster's interpretation.

The Luveniwai, or Water Babies, who inhabited an island in the Rewa River delta, were believed to have originated from miscarriages of ladies of rank. Such is often the origin of spirits not only in Melanesia but in Polynesia, where Maui is the outstanding example.[3] Orokaivans of New Guinea believe in comparable little creatures, the Hovatu-koiari, who are about one foot high and have a long tail hanging from their navel. They are spirits of stillborn children, who live in the swamps and cry pitifully for their mothers (Williams, 74, p. 278).

Secret societies of young Fijian men endeavoured to lure the timid Water Babies from the sea to the woodland, where votaries of the society, called Kalourere in some parts and Ndomindomi in others, were assembled in the hope that a sprite would enter one of them. Such spirit possession conferred

---

[3] See Luomala, Katharine, "Maui-of-a-thousand-tricks: His Oceanic and European Biographers," B. P. Bishop Mus., Bull. 198, 1949.

distinction on the chosen individual, and he might be able to gain importance in his tribe as a result.

The Veli and the Water Babies taught their human followers songs, rituals, and dances, and conferred on them immunity from wounds. But mostly the cults provided an outlet for restless and rebellious young men who used the "little gods" from the water and the forests as their supernatural sponsors. The missionaries and native elders eventually requested governmental action against the headstrong youths, some of whom were officially flogged as an example to their companions. As a substitute activity, the members were organized into cricket clubs—complete with scarlet uniforms, titles, and badges—but then the elders began to suspect that the cricket clubs were simply disguises for the old Water Babies Society and that the members were using the cloak of the English game to cover up their old habits of making magic and raising hell.

According to Brewster, in Tholo East district in Viti Levu, the term Luveniwai came to have less the significance of Water Babies and more that of woodland spirits or fauns like the Veli. The Veli, like the Water Babies, were little and handsome. They lived in hollow trees or caves and dugouts in the woods and had kava, their own bananas, and other wild plants, some of which are now cultivated. One of Williams' native informants states that the little gods used "to assemble in troops on the top of the mountains, and sing unweariedly"; he had seen them often and repeated one of their songs to Williams. Although some of the woodland spirits were malevolent, Brewster states that the water sprites were a friendly little folk. They are not connected with any stonework except in so far as members of the Water Babies Society sometimes made jetties of stones to encourage the spirits to come onto land. Cairns of stones accumulated in regions where woodland spirits lurked, for travelers left stones as offerings to them.

Apparently, there is a common tradition throughout these areas about odd, semi-human people, many of them very small. Each locality reinterprets the common stock of tales, fits them into its folklore, and renames the bands and re-localizes the events.

The Polynesian, Micronesian, and Melanesian bands of little people described above represent merely a sampling of the available material.

SUMMARY

Like the Hawaiian Menehune, bands of legendary beings in New Zealand, Micronesia, and Melanesia are regarded by Europeans and natives as aborigines of less than pygmy size who built the earthworks, stonework, and natural features of the landscape in their islands. The Patupaiarehe of New Zealand, the Chokalai of Ponape, the Malavui of the Banks Islands, and the Masi and the Kakamora of the Solomons have much the same folklore function as that of the Menehune; and the same mythological processes of change are observable. There is no trustworthy evidence that they were the first settlers of their land, or even folklorized real people of a later period.

These bands of spirits or semi-human characters are being absorbed into a stereotype which is thereby elaborated by their inclusion. Distinctions between bands are being blurred, and explanations are being invented to reconcile the differences. The stupid Masi are beginning to be described as tiny like the Kakamora, whereas the latter are beginning to get the reputation of being artisans like the Masi. The coastal Water Babies, spirits of miscarriages, have become partly identified with the Veli, woodland spirits who live in the interior of the island, but as yet neither band has been regarded by a storyteller as related to the mythical little builders of the *nanga,* the ceremonial stone structures in the area. Conflicting opinions exist about the size of the Patupaiarehe, some narrators calling them normal-sized, others describing them as tiny.

The tiny size of the members of certain bands seems to me to represent a quality especially peculiar to the forest spirits, perhaps because, as in New Zealand, they are sometimes represented as the personification of insects and other small life of the woods. There is probably no single categorical answer to account for each instance of spirit bands being described as tiny. However, from the storyteller's viewpoint, exaggeration helps make a story better. Characters then become giants or pygmies. When it comes to thinking up an explanation for stonework of forgotten origin, which makes a better story, the giants who lift great stones like pebbles or the little people whose magic, cooperation, and ingenuity make up for what they lack in strength? Early Americans preferred characters like the giant Paul Bunyan. The Oceanic peoples apparently prefer to have little people perform stupendous and miraculous tasks, as the giants who do figure in the stories are usually stupid cannibals. Here, again, the contrast between size and brains makes a good story, for a smart, little child can outwit a stupid, cannibalistic giant in Oceanic myths. Once the mythic pattern was established for clever, little people and stupid giants it persisted. A historical element forming part of the complex of factors producing the pattern in the Society Islands is the fact that the Manahune laborers tended to be thinner and more wiry than the large, corpulent chiefs and their families who regarded fat and height as aesthetically admirable and proof of royal blood.

Storytellers in many parts of the world have in their repertoires tales about little people who seem to share many of the same habits and qualities as the Oceanic mites. Often they are believed to have preceded the present inhabitants of a region and to have been a race apart from them. Such is the belief among the Ainu of Japan about a race of little people, "Earth Spiders," whom subsequent scientific research has suggested to be the ancestors of the Ainu themselves, folklorized and made exaggeratedly small by later narrators. The name pixies for little people of England is said to have been derived from the name,

Picts, a people whose modified name in the course of time became only a peg for storytellers to hang their fancies on. In the first case, the forgotten ancestors were given a new name descriptive of their underground life in pit dwellings, comparatively few of which were made in later Ainu culture. In the second case, an old name has been modified slightly to describe fairy folk. In the case of the Hawaiian Menehune, a foreign name has been applied to a kind of fairy folk whose role was inspired by the working-class connotation of this name. There is nothing to prove, either in the Society or Cook Islands or in the Hawaiian Islands, that the name ever meant aborigine or *kama'aina* before Hawaiian storytellers absorbed the Menehune into the stereotyped pattern of strange, forest spirits and ascribed to them first possession of the land.

Wild men, real human beings who were war refugees or were social outcasts for other reasons, have also contributed material to the Oceanic mythology about forest bands. They wander about only at night, live a simple life, hide in the mountainous interior of islands, have neither fire nor cooked food, are unkempt, long-haired, and ferocious-looking, and steal at night from travelers. Haunting the forests, they seem to be its guardians and may alternately help or frighten travelers. They blend into the stock type of forest beings who are invisible (except to gifted human beings), work only at night, fear daylight, and have supernormal powers. Local factors vary the stereotype. For instance, the Maori usually describe their forest bands as having golden or red hair. They are fair people unlike the Hawaiian bands, whom narrators describe as dark, awkward, and dwarfish, with amazing strength.

CONCLUSION

The name of Menehune probably reached the Hawaiian Islands from central Polynesia, where it is known, with dialectical variations, in the Society, Cook, and Tuamotuan Archipelagoes. Whatever its special local application in each of these groups, it bears the connotation of plebeian; and in Tahiti, is applied to the lower class. Hawaiians, however, at least since the time of discovery, have called their plebeians Makaainana, the term used in the Marquesas. Hawaiians reserve the term Menehune for bands of supernatural, night-working artisans of very small height who specialize in stonework and live a simple life in the mountainous interiors of the islands, especially of Kauai. Actually, the Makaainana performed the labor on the stone heiaus and fishponds, but as Hawaiian culture altered under the influence of white contact and the histories of many stone structures were forgotten, the mythical Menehune were credited with the construction. The process of attributing such work to the Menehune as more and more history is forgotten is observable today.

Storytellers, to hold the interest of their listeners, elaborated the description of the Menehune and their customs and ignored their prosaic, normal-sized counterparts, the Makaainana. The supernatural aspect of the Menehune traditions was enriched by additions from the stock-in-trade of beliefs about other forest-dwelling beings of supernatural qualities, and these beings gained a little too by being pitted against Menehune and taking on some of their peculiarities. One of the most interesting details in the description of the Menehune is their low height of two or three feet. I believe that several factors have entered into the formation of this detail: (1) storytellers' genius for exaggeration; (2) their assimilation of the Menehune to the stereotyped concept of forest spirits; and (3) the comparatively smaller size of many lower class workers, such as the Tahitian Manahune, which resulted from their less favorable diet and living conditions.

Comparison of the Hawaiian Menehune tradition with beliefs and myths about other strange, mythical bands of wonder-working little people elsewhere in Polynesia, Micronesia, and Melanesia reveals that native narrators in these three culture areas follow the same general pattern in the attributes assigned these bands. There is nothing to prove that they were ever real people. They are the products of human imagination, and considering the lack of any good evidence to the contrary, the only conclusion possible is that they are mythical people invented by storytellers who have added to their stock-in-trade the inventions of their colleagues until the present common pattern of belief about little people has emerged in Oceania.

BIBLIOGRAPHY

1. ADAMS, HENRY (editor), Memoirs of Arii Taimai, Paris, 1901.
2. BEAGLEHOLE, ERNEST AND PEARL, Ethnology of Pukapuka: B. P. Bishop Mus., Bull. 150, 1938.
3. BEATTIE, HERRIES, Traditions and legends: Polynesian Soc., Jour., vol. 28, 1919.
4. BECKWITH, MARTHA W. (editor), Kepelino's traditions of Hawaii: B. P. Bishop Mus., Bull. 95, 1932.
5. BECKWITH, MARTHA W., Hawaiian mythology, New Haven, Connecticut, 1940.
6. BENNETT, W. C., Archaeology of Kauai: B. P. Bishop Mus., Bull. 80, 1931.
7. BEST, ELSDON, Tuhoe: Polynesian Soc., Mem., vol. 6, 1925.
8. BLACKWOOD, BEATRICE, Both sides of Buka Passage, Oxford, 1935.
9. BOUGAINVILLE, L. A., DE, A voyage round the world . . . translated by J. R. Forster, London, 1772.
10. BOVIS, DE, État de la société Taitienne . . ., Papeete, 1909.
11. BREWSTER, A. B., The hill tribes of Fiji, Philadelphia, 1922.
12. BUCK, P. H. (TE RANGI HIROA), Mangaian society: B. P. Bishop Mus., Bull. 122, 1934.
13. BUCK, P. H. (TE RANGI HIROA), Vikings of the sunrise, New York, 1938.
14. BUCK, P. H. (TE RANGI HIROA), The Hawaiians arrive in Hawaii: Paradise of the Pacific, vol. 51, no. 12, Honolulu, 1939.
15. BUCK, P. H. (TE RANGI HIROA), Arts and crafts of the Cook Islands: B. P. Bishop Mus., Bull. 179, 1944.
16. BURROWS, E. G., Ethnology of Futuna: B. P. Bishop Mus., Bull. 138, 1936.
17. BURROWS, E. G., Ethnology of Uvea (Wallis Island): B. P. Bishop Mus., Bull. 145, 1937.
18. CHRISTIAN, F. W., The Caroline Islands, London, 1899.
19. CODRINGTON, R. H., The Melanesians, studies in their anthropology and folk-lore, Oxford, 1891.
20. COWAN, JAMES, The Patu-Paiarehe: Polynesian Soc., Jour., vol. 30, 1931.
21. ELLIS, WILLIAM, Polynesian researches, vols. 1 and 3, London, 1853.
22. EMORY, K. P., Footprints in Maui lava flows: Paradise of the Pacific, vol. 35, no. 7, Honolulu, 1922.
23. EMORY, K. P., The island of Lanai: B. P. Bishop Mus., Bull. 12, 1924.
24. EMORY, K. P., Archaeology of Nihoa and Necker Islands: B. P. Bishop Mus., Bull. 53, 1928.
25. ERDLAND, P. A., Die Marshall-insulaner, Munster, 1914.
26. FORNANDER, ABRAHAM, An account of the Polynesian race, vols. 1-3, London, 1878-1895.
27. FORNANDER, ABRAHAM, Collection of Hawaiian antiquities and folk-lore: B. P. Bishop Mus., Mem., vol. 6, pts. 1 and 2, 1919.
28. FORSTER, J. R., Observations made during a voyage round the world . . . London, 1778.
29. FOX, C. E., Threshold of the Pacific, New York, 1925.
30. GILL, WILLIAM W., Historical sketches of savage life in Polynesia, Wellington, 1880.
31. GREEN, LAURA, Folk-tales from Hawaii, Poughkeepsie, 1926.
32. GREY, GEORGE, Polynesian mythology, Auckland, 1929.

33. HAMBRUCH, PAUL, Ponape: IN Thilenius, Georg, Ergebnisse der Südsee-Expedition 1908-1910. II. Ethnographie: B. Micronesien, vol. 7, pt. 1, Hamburg, 1932; pt. 3, Hamburg, 1936.

34. HANDY, E. S. C., History and culture in the Society Islands: B. P. Bishop Mus., Bull. 79, 1930.

35. HANDY, E. S. C., The problem of Polynesian origins: B. P. Bishop Mus., Occ. Papers, vol. 9, no. 8, 1930.

36. HENRY, TEUIRA, Ancient Tahiti: B. P. Bishop Mus., Bull. 48, 1928.

37. HOFGAARD, C. B., Who were the Menehunes?: Paradise of the Pacific, vol. 41, no. 4, Honolulu, 1928.

38. HUGHES, GWLADYS F., Folk beliefs and customs in an Hawaiian community: Jour. Am. Folklore, vol. 62, pp. 294-311, 1949.

39. IVENS, W. G., Melanesians of the southeast Solomon Islands, London, 1927.

40. IVENS, W. G., The island builders of the Pacific, London, 1930.

41. JOHNSTONE, ARTHUR, Storied Nuuanu: Hawaiian Annual for 1908.

42. KAIWI, J. H., Story of the race of Menehunes of Kauai: Hawaiian Annual for 1921. (Also printed in Polynesian Soc. Jour., vol. 28, 1919.)

43. LINTON, RALPH, Archaeology of the Marquesas Islands: B. P. Bishop Mus., Bull. 23, 1925.

44. LYDGATE, JOHN M., The affairs of the Wainiha Hui: Hawaiian Annual for 1913.

45. LYDGATE, JOHN M., The winning of the Mu-ai-maia maiden: Hawaiian Hist. Soc., Ann. Rept., 1920.

46. LYDGATE, JOHN M., Legend of the floating island: Hawaiian Annual for 1924.

47. McALLISTER, J. G., Archaeology of Oahu: B. P. Bishop Mus., Bull. 104, 1933.

48. MAHONY, B. G., Legends of the Niua Islands: Polynesian Soc., Jour., vol. 24, 1915.

49. MALO, DAVID, Hawaiian antiquities, 1st ed., Honolulu, 1903.

50. Polynesian Soc., Jour., editorial notes inserted into articles, vol. 28, 1919; vol. 29, 1920; a review, vol. 30, 1921.

51. Polynesian Soc., Jour., The Manahune people, vol. 30, 1921.

52. RICE, WILLIAM HYDE, Hawaiian legends: B. P. Bishop Mus., Bull. 3, 1923.

53. RIVERS, W. H. R., The history of Melanesian society, 2 vols., Cambridge, 1914.

54. SCHERZER, KARL, Narrative of the circumnavigation of the globe, vol. 3, London, 1863.

55. SHAND, ALEXANDER, The Moriori people of the Chatham Islands, Polynesian Soc., Jour., vol. 3, 1894.

56. STOKES, J. F. G., Whence Paao?: Hawaiian Hist. Soc., Papers, no. 15, 1928.

57. TE ARIKI-TARA-ARE, History and traditions of Rarotonga, Polynesian Soc., Jour., vol. 28, no. 112, 1919.

58. TEFAAFANA, TETUAA, La legende des pierres marchantes (Ofaitere) de Papetoai, Soc. d'Etudes Océaniennes, Bull. 1, p. 31, 1917.

59. THOMPSON, LAURA M., Archaeology of the Marianas Islands: B. P. Bishop Mus., Bull. 100, 1932.

60. THOMSON, BASIL, The Fijians, London, 1908.

61. THRUM, T. G., Manoa Valley: Hawaiian Annual for 1892.

62. THRUM, T. G., Stories of the Menehune: Hawaiian Annual for 1895.

63. THRUM, T. G., Hawaiian folk tales, Chicago, 1907.

64. THRUM, T. G., Tales from the temples: Hawaiian Annual for 1907 and 1909.

65. THRUM, T. G., Heiaus and heiau sites throughout the Hawaiian Islands: Hawaiian Annual for 1907 and 1909.

66. THRUM, T. G., Hawaiian traditions: Stories of the Menehunes, Chicago, 1910.

67. THRUM, T. G., The legend of Kanehuna-moku: Hawaiian Annual for 1916.

68. THRUM, T. G., More Hawaiian folk tales, Chicago, 1923.

69. THRUM, T. G., Heiaus (temples) of Hawaii Nei: Hawaiian Hist. Soc., Ann. Rept., 1923.

70. THRUM, T. G., Who or what were the Menehunes: Hawaiian Annual for 1929.

71. WESTERVELT, W. D., Legends of gods and ghosts, Boston and London, 1915.

72. WESTERVELT, W. D., Legends of old Honolulu, Boston and London, 1915.

73. WHITE, JOHN, Ancient history of the Maori, vol. 3, Wellington, 1887.

74. WILLIAMS, F. E., Orokaiva society, London, 1930.

75. WILLIAMS, THOMAS, Fiji and the Fijians, vol. 1, London, 1860.

76. WILLIAMSON, ROBERT W., The social and political systems of Central Polynesia, vol. 2, Cambridge, 1924.

77. WILLIAMSON, ROBERT W., Essays in Polynesian ethnology, edited by Ralph Piddington, Cambridge, 1939.

78. WILSON, JAMES, A missionary voyage to the southern Pacific Ocean . . . in the ship Duff . . ., London, 1799.

INDEX

Coachwhip Publications

CoachwhipBooks.com

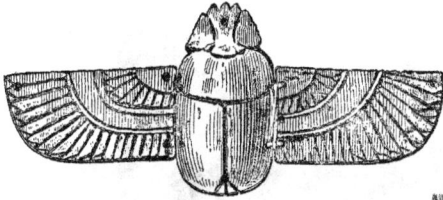

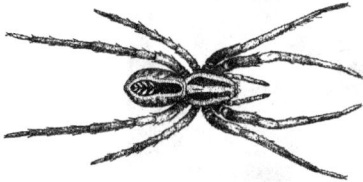

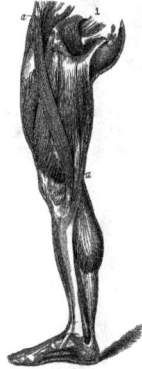

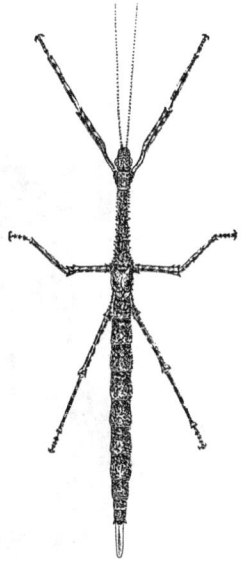

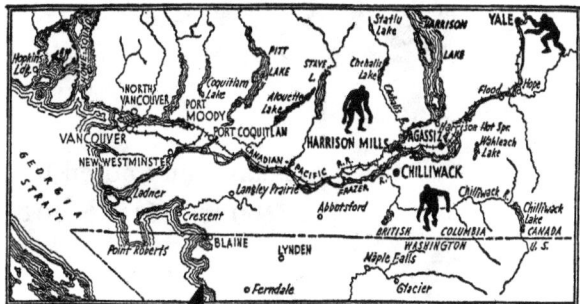

ALASKAN
TEN
FOOTED
BEAR

AND OTHER LEGENDS

Compiled by RUTH McCORKLE
Illustrated by WILBUR WALLUK

Alaskan Ten Footed Bear
ISBN 978-1-61646-201-7

ALASKAN
IGLOO TALES

Edward L. Keithahn

Illustrated by
George Aden Ahgupuk

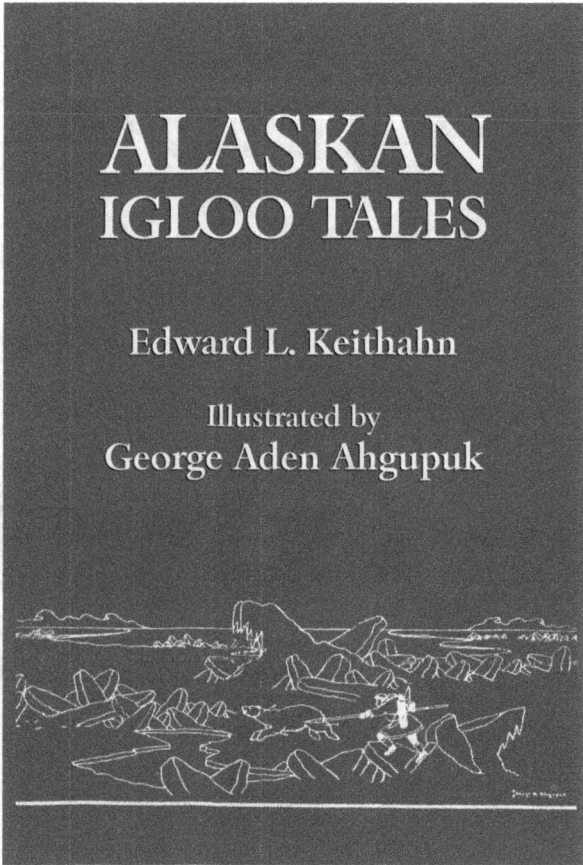

Alaskan Igloo Tales
ISBN 978-1-61646-199-7

COACHWHIP PUBLICATIONS

ALSO AVAILABLE

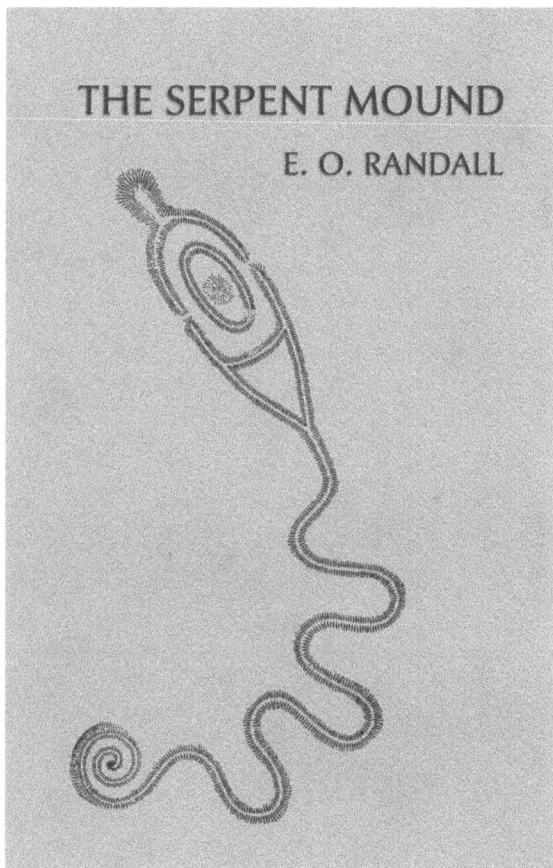

THE SERPENT MOUND

E. O. RANDALL

The Serpent Mound
ISBN 978-1-61646-167-6

www.ingramcontent.com/pod-product-compliance
Lightning Source LLC
Chambersburg PA
CBHW070811280326
41934CB00012B/3155